How t Micr PowerPc

Other Titles of Interest

BP476　Microsoft PowerPoint 2000 Explained

BP477　Using Microsoft FrontPage 2000

BP480　A Practical Introduction to Sage Line 50

BP482　Sage Instant Accounting 2000

BP490　Web Pages using Microsoft Office 2000

BP492　A Practical Introduction To Microsoft Office 2000

BP497　Microsoft Outlook 2000 explained

BP519　How to use Norton SystemWorks 2002

How to Use Microsoft PowerPoint 2002

David Weale

**Bernard Babani (Publishing) Ltd
The Grampians
Shepherds Bush Road
London W6 7NF
England**

www.babanibooks.com

Please Note

Although every care has been taken with the production of this book to ensure that any instructions or any of the other contents operate in a correct and safe manner, the Author and the Publishers do not accept any responsibility for any failure, damage or loss caused by following the said contents. The Author and Publisher do not take any responsibility for errors or omissions.

The Author and Publisher make no warranty or representation, either express or implied, with respect to the contents of this book, its quality, merchantability or fitness for a particular purpose.

The Author and Publisher will not be liable to the purchaser or to any other person or legal entity with respect to any liability, loss or damage (whether direct, indirect, special, incidental or consequential) caused or alleged to be caused directly or indirectly by this book.

The book is sold as is, without any warranty of any kind, either expressed or implied, respecting the contents, including but not limited to implied warranties regarding the book's quality, performance, correctness or fitness for any particular purpose.

No part of this book may be reproduced or copied by any means whatever without written permission of the publisher.

All rights reserved

© 2002 BERNARD BABANI (publishing) LTD

First Published – May 2002

British Library Cataloguing in Publication Data

A catalogue record for this book is available from the British Library

ISBN 0 85934 524 6

Cover Design by Gregor Arthur

Printed and bound in Great Britain by Guernsey Press

Preface

Welcome, I wrote this book to help you in learning how to use the program in a practical way. It is intended to explain the program in a way that I hope you will find useful, and that you will learn by doing.

Each section of the book covers a different aspect of the program and contains various hints and tips which I have found useful and may enhance your work.

The text is written both for the new user and for the more experienced person who wants an easy to follow reference.

You should know how to use the basic techniques of Microsoft® Windows®; if you do not, there are many excellent texts on the subject.

I hope you learn from this book and have fun doing so.

David Weale, March 2002

Trademarks

Microsoft®, Windows® and Windows® XP are registered trademarks of Microsoft ® Corporation.

All other trademarks are the registered and legally protected trademarks of the companies who make the products. There is no intent to use the trademarks generally and readers should investigate ownership of a trademark before using it for any purpose.

About the author

David Weale is a Fellow of the Institute of Chartered Accountants and has worked in both private and public practice. At present, he is a lecturer in business computing.

Contents

STARTING OFF 1

The display *1*
   The default screen 1
   The toolbars 2
   The panes 4
      Removing the panes 6
   The pull down menus 6

Starting a new presentation *7*
   Blank Presentation 7
   From Design Template 9
   AutoContent Wizard 10

New from existing presentation *12*

New from template *13*
   General Templates 13
   Templates on my web sites 13
   Templates on microsoft.com 14

Adding a new slide *14*

Moving between slides *15*

Changing the design *16*

Color Scheme *17*

Looking at Your Slides *18*
   Normal 19
      Sizing the panes 19
      Zooming 19

Slide Sorter View *20*

- *Slide Show* *21*
  - The Slide Show menu 22
    - Next/Previous/Go 22
    - Slide Navigator/By Title 23
    - Custom Show 23
    - Meeting Minder 24
    - Speaker Notes 25
    - Pointer Options 26
    - Screen/End Show 27
- *Printing* *28*
  - Print what 28
    - Slides 29
    - Handouts 29
    - Notes Pages 29
    - Outline View 29
    - Scale to fit paper 30
    - Frame slides 30
    - Include comment pages 30
    - Print hidden slides 30
- *Saving Your Work* *31*
- **TEXT** **33**
  - *Entering Text* *33*
    - Altering the Font 34
    - Spell Checking Your Text 35
  - *Graphics & Objects* *36*
  - *ClipArt* *37*
    - Pictures, sounds and videos 40
  - *Graphs* *41*
  - *WordArt* *44*
  - *Tables* *46*
    - Creating tables within PowerPoint 46

- *Organisation Charts* *51*
  - Organization Chart Toolbar 54
  - Insert Shape 54
  - Layout 55
  - Select 55
  - AutoFormat 56
- *Other Objects* *57*
- **ARTWORK** **59**
  - *Manipulating Images* *59*
    - Moving an Image (or Other Object) 59
    - Sizing an Image 59
    - Cropping an Object 61
- **CUSTOMISING SLIDES** **63**
  - *The Master Slide* *63*
  - *Deleting Slides* *65*
  - *Drawing toolbar* *66*
    - Draw 66
      - Grouping and Ungrouping 67
      - Merging images 68
      - Superimposing One Image on Another 69
    - Order 69
      - Bring to Front 70
      - Send to Back 70
      - Bring Forward 70
      - Send Backward 70
    - Grid and Guides 71
    - Nudge 72
    - Align or Distribute 72
    - Rotate or Flip 73
      - Rotating Text 74
    - Edit Points 74

Change AutoShape	74
AutoShapes	*75*
POWERPOINT AND THE WEB	**77**
Saving a presentation as HTML	77
Web file structure	80
Adding hyperlinks	80
THE PULL DOWN MENUS	**83**
File menu	*84*
Search	85
Pack and Go	86
Web Page Preview	87
Page Setup	87
Print Preview	88
Send To	89
Mail Recipient	89
Routing Recipient	90
Exchange Folder	90
Microsoft Word	91
Properties	92
Edit menu	*93*
Cut, Copy and Paste	93
Office Clipboard	94
Paste Special	95
Paste as Hyperlink	95
Clear	96
Select All	96
Duplicate	96
Delete Slide	96
Find	97
Replace	97
Go to Property	98

Links	98
Objects/Text	98

View menu *99*

Color/Grayscale	99
Toolbars	100
Rulers	101
Grid and Guides	102
Header and Footer	103
Markup	105

Insert menu *106*

Duplicate Slide	106
Slide Number / Date and Time	106
Symbol	107
Comment	107
Slides from Files	108
Slides from Outline	109
Pictures	110
Text Box	112
Movies and Sounds	113

Format menu *116*

Font	116
Bullets and Numbering	117
Alignment	118
Line Spacing	119
Change Case	120
Replacing Fonts	121
Slide Design	121
Background	122
Format Text/Object/Picture/Placeholder	123
Format Painter	123
Tools menu	124

Language 124
Speech 125
Compare and Merge Presentations 125
Online Collaboration 127
Meeting Minder 127
Tools on the Web 127
Macro 128
    Recording and running a macro 128
    Assigning a macro to a toolbar button 129
    Running a macro during a slide show 130
Add-Ins 130
AutoCorrect Options 131
Customize 132
Options 134

Slide Show Menu *135*

View Show 135
Set Up Show 136
Rehearse Timings 136
Record Narration 137
Online broadcast 138
Action Buttons 138
Action Settings 140
Animation Schemes 141
Custom Animation 142
    Dimming text 143
Slide Transition 145
Hide Slide 146
    Displaying Hidden Slides 146
Custom Shows 147

- *Help menu* *148*
  - The Office Assistant 148
    - Choices 148
    - The Search Button 149
    - Using the Show button 151
  - Office on the Web 153
  - Detect and Repair 154
  - About Microsoft PowerPoint 154
- **ADVICE ABOUT PRESENTATIONS** **155**
  - First Things 155
  - The Material 155
  - The Presentation 156
  - The Environment Itself 157
  - Using Software 157
  - Slide Layout 158
- **INDEX** **161**

Starting Off

The display

When you load **Microsoft® PowerPoint** for the first time, you will see the screen shown below.

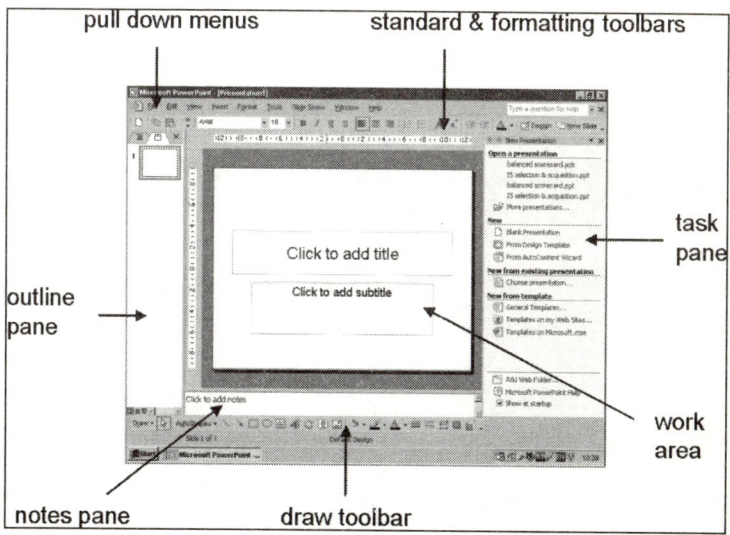

The default screen

The **Standard**, **Formatting** and **Draw** toolbar(s) contain buttons, which you click to carry out activities or commands.

The default setting is to display a single line of toolbar buttons at the top of the screen, plus the **Draw** toolbar along the bottom of the screen, the **Task Pane** toolbar to the right of the screen, the **Outline** pane to the left and the **Notes** pane along the bottom of the screen.

To display any toolbar, pull down the **View** menu, select **Toolbars** and then the chosen toolbar.

The toolbars

You may wish to show the **Standard** & **Formatting** toolbar buttons in two rows.

To achieve this, click the arrow (**Toolbar Options**) at the end of the toolbar and select **Show Buttons on Two Rows.**

The display will change to show two lines of toolbars.

The toolbar buttons are an alternative to using the pull down menus and you can add or remove buttons as you wish (to add or remove buttons, pull down the **Tools** menu and select **Customize**).

If you position the mouse pointer over any of the toolbar buttons, a description will appear (called **ScreenTips**, this is an option that can be turned off if you wish – **Tools, Customize, Options**).

If you click the right-hand mouse button while pointing at any button a pull-down menu containing the available toolbars will appear enabling you to display those you wish to see.

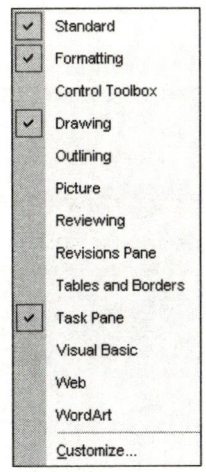

The panes

There are various panes to assist you in making various choices.

The **Outline** pane (left of the screen) displays a small representation of each slide *or* the outline text for each slide (switch between these views using the buttons at the top of the pane).

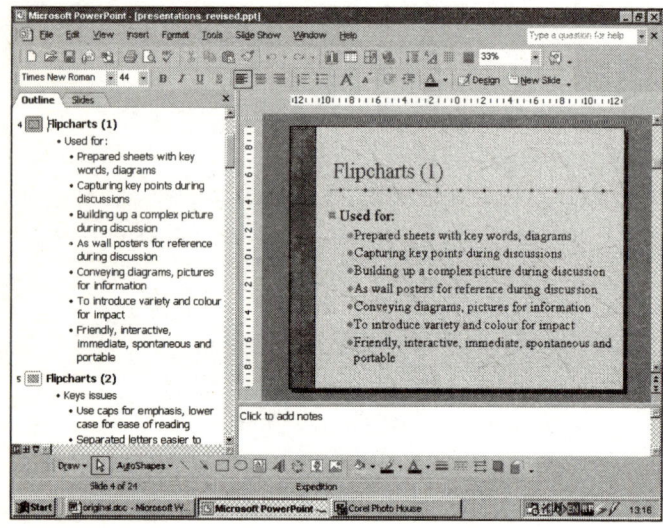

The **Task** pane (on the right of the screen) displays common tasks that can be carried out by clicking the appropriate item, this display changes with the activity and enables you to select the task from those displayed (at each stage of the creation of the presentation).

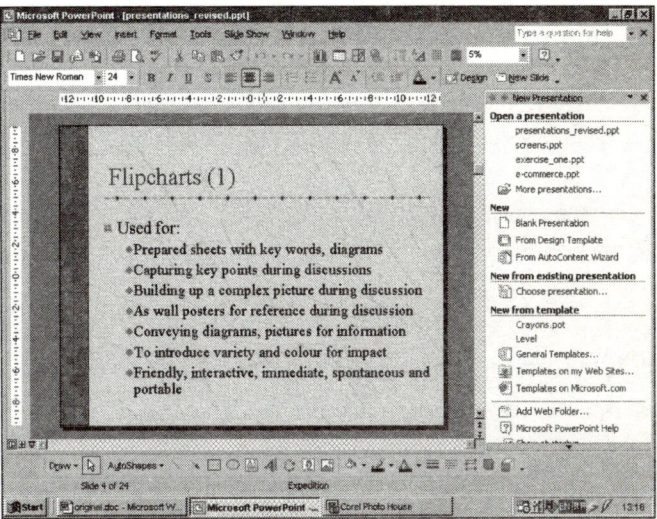

The pane can only display the most used tasks due to space and it may be necessary to use the pull down menus and toolbar buttons.

Note the arrows at the top of the pane, these can be used to move backwards and forwards between the different views of the **Task** pane.

The **Notes** pane is useful, type text that you want to use to help you within your presentation, i.e. prompts, details, etc.

The **Notes** can be printed out (using **Print** within the **File** menu) and used when the presentation takes place.

Removing the panes

The **Outline** and **Task** panes can be removed by clicking the **X** button (on the top right of pane).

The **Notes** pane (bottom of screen) can be resized by clicking and dragging the divide along the top of the pane.

To restore the panes, pull down the **View** menu and select **Normal (Restore Panes)** followed by **Task Pane** from the same list.

The pull down menus

Along the top of the screen are the pull-down menus.

File Edit View Insert Format Tools Slide Show Window Help

When you click the (left) mouse button on any of these, a pull-down menu will appear.

Each contains several related commands (some of which can also be carried out using the toolbar buttons). These are dealt with later in the book.

Starting a new presentation

Pulling down the **File** menu, followed by **New** will begin a new presentation.

There are four choices (shown in the pane on the right of the screen).

We will look at each in turn.

Blank Presentation

The initial option is the blank presentation. This gives you a choice of layouts (in the **Task** pane on the right of the screen) without the addition of a design.

There is a variety of different types of layouts (the chosen layout can be changed at any time by pulling down the **Format** menu and selecting **Slide Layout**).

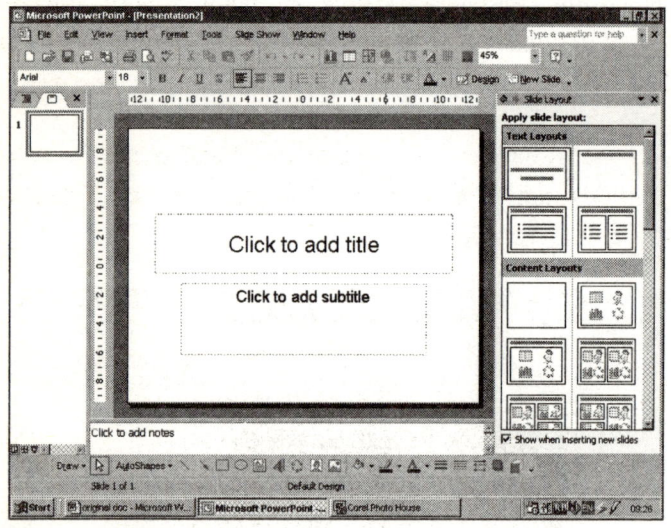

This is an ideal choice if you wish to apply a design at a later stage.

From Design Template

It is a sensible idea to select the design early in the process of designing your slide show as each design imposes colour schemes and font choices, which may affect the contents of each slide.

Use the scrollbar on the right of the **Task** pane to see all the choices and select one by clicking it; it will then be imposed onto your slide(s).

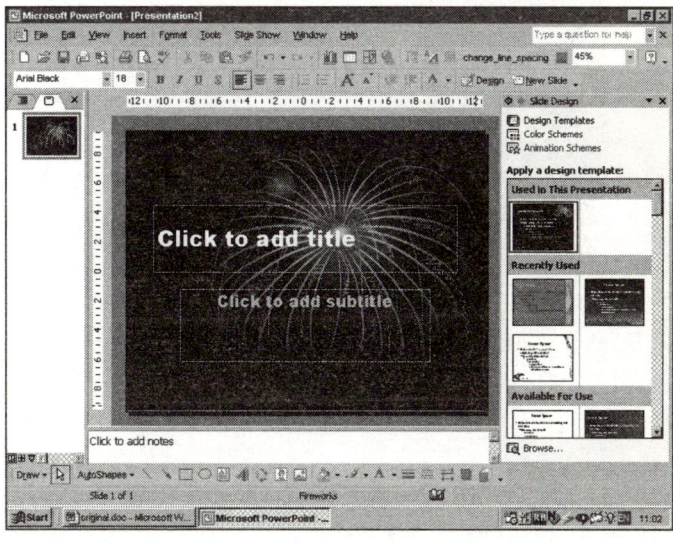

Right clicking any of the designs gives three choices, **Show Large Previews** can be useful to enable more clarity and the design can be applied to the current slide or to all the slides.

AutoContent Wizard

This guides you through a series of steps. You enter various details or make choices in each. The result is a professional presentation that you can create in a very short time.

The first screen is shown below.

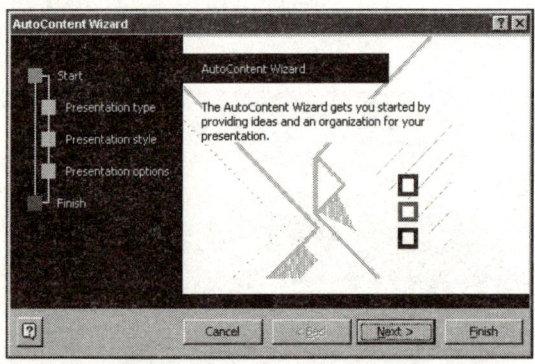

This is followed by a series of other screens, the content of which will differ depending upon your choices at each stage.

As you can see from the next screens, there are varieties of different presentation wizards to choose (including web page presentations that can be put onto the Internet or your organisation's Intranet).

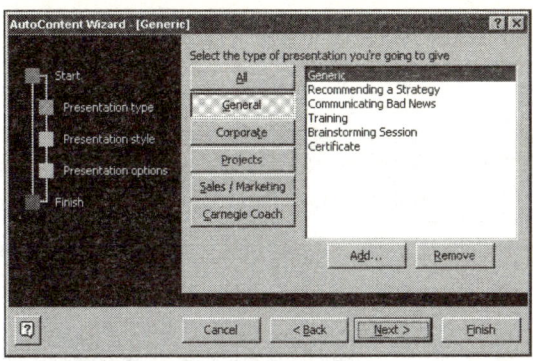
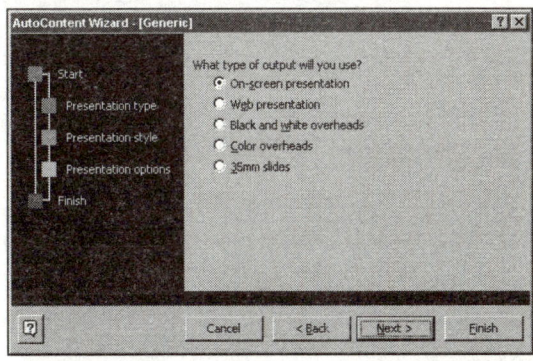
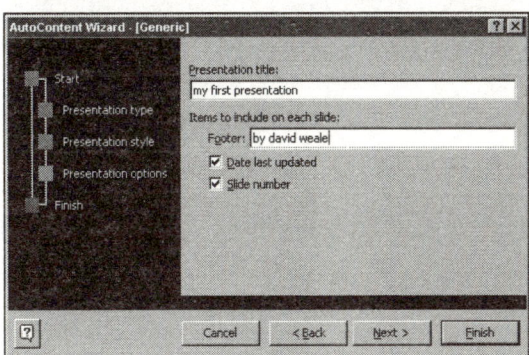

When you have finished, the Wizard leaves you with a presentation with prompting text already in place.

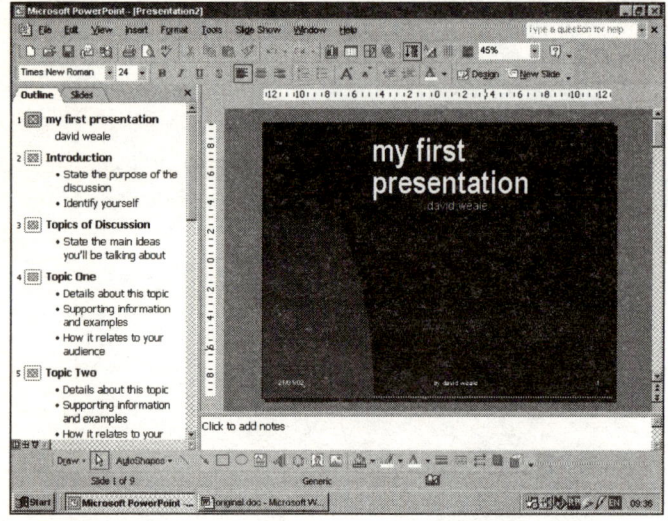

All you have to do is to alter the text (by highlighting and overwriting) to whatever you want to say.

You can add or delete slides as you wish.

New from existing presentation

This means using an existing slide show as the basis for the new presentations, the existing file will be opened and then you can add or delete slides, change the content, design, etc.

New from template

There are three choices.

General Templates

This displays a choice of templates (within a dialog box rather than within the **Task** pane); select one of these and it will be imposed onto your slide show.

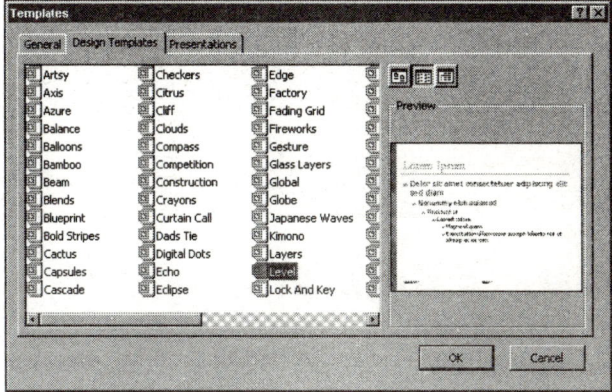

This is alternative to the earlier option (**From Design Template**).

Templates on my web sites

Using this option, you can look for templates on web sites in the same way you would look on your hard disc.

13

Templates on microsoft.com

This connects to the Microsoft web site and looks for new templates to incorporate into your presentation. Click on the appropriate destination and the browser will be redirected to the relevant site and page.

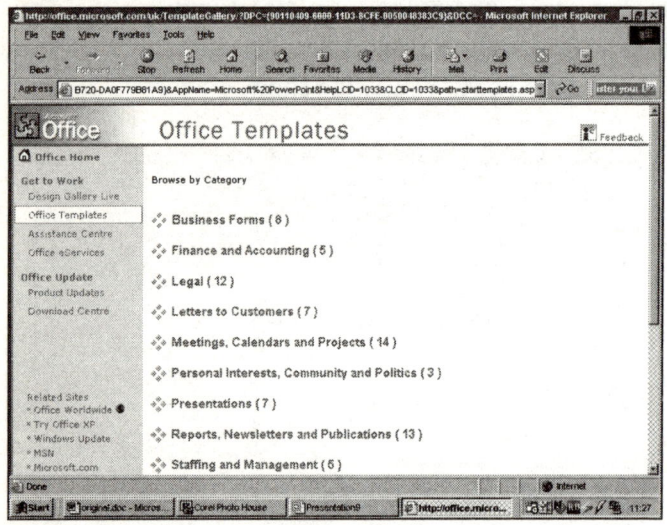

Adding a new slide

Use the **New Slide** button (on the toolbar) to add a new slide (which will appear after the current slide).

Alternatively, pull down the **Insert** menu and select **New Slide**, or use the keys **Ctrl** and **M** to achieve the same result.

Moving between slides

There are several ways to move from one slide to another.

- Click the required slide in the **Outline** pane (to the left of the screen).
- Use the keyboard **Pg Up** and **Pg Dn**.
- Use the scroll-bar to the right of the actual slide.

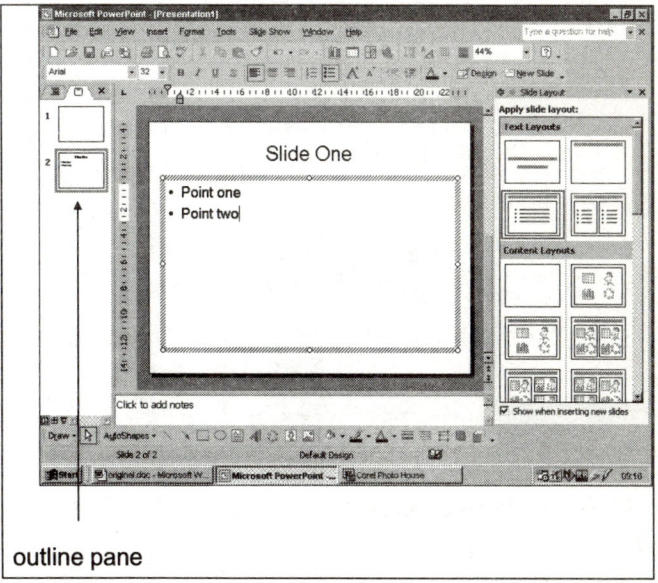

outline pane

Changing the design

Click the **Design** button (on the **Formatting** toolbar) to display the **Slide Design** pane on the right of the screen.

This will display both the current choice and the other variations (use the scrollbar to move through the choices).

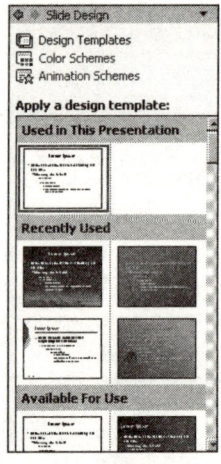

The **Slide Design** pane also enables the **Color Scheme** and **Animation Scheme** to be changed (animations are covered later in the text).

Color Scheme

The choice of designs is shown in the right-hand pane. Moving the mouse pointer over any of them displays an arrow (on the right of the colour scheme), clicking this enables the colour scheme to be applied.

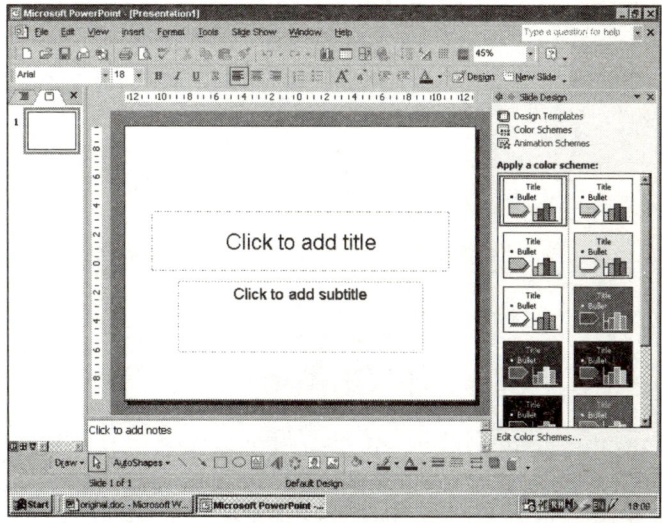

There are three choices, **Show Large Previews** can be useful to enable more clarity and the colour scheme can be applied to the current slide or to all the slides.

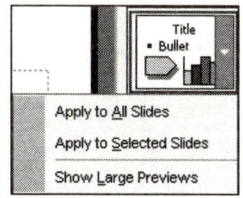

There is also an **Edit Color Schemes** link at the bottom of the pane (this loads a dialogue box from which the colours can be changed by choosing the colour and then clicking the **Change Color** button).

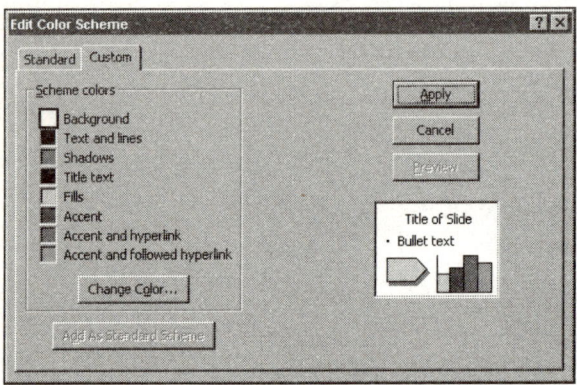

Looking at Your Slides

Along the bottom left of the screen are three buttons enabling the slides to be looked at in different ways (there are further views available from the **View** pull-down menu).

From left to right the buttons are **Normal** view, **Slide Sorter** view and **Slide Show** view.

Normal

The default view and the view you use to create the slides.

Sizing the panes

The panes can be sized (click and drag the divider between the sections of the screen) and closed (using the **Close** button that appears top right on every window).

Zooming

To size (*any*) display, click the **Zoom Control** button on the upper toolbar.

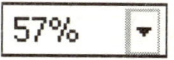

Alternatively, pull down the **View** menu and choose **Zoom**, this gives more control as you can enter a figure in the **Percent** box.

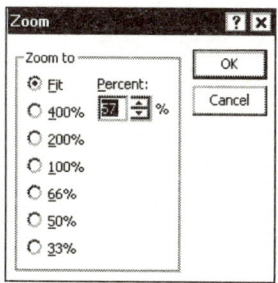

Slide Sorter View

You can look at all the slides by clicking on the **Slide Sorter View** button (along the bottom of the screen).

You will see the following display.

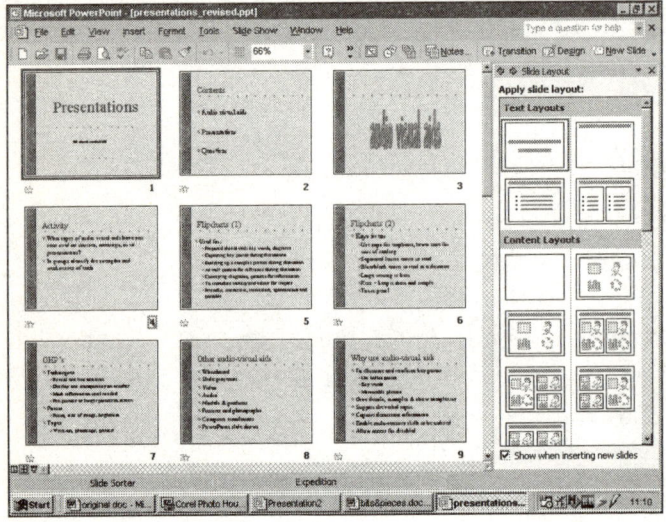

This displays (small) images of all your slides and you can rearrange the sequence or add/delete slides.

To move the slides around, click on a slide with the mouse and then drag it to a new position (between two slides, a line will appear between the slides).

You can **Select All** from the **Edit** menu and apply special effects such as **Transitions** to all the slides (using the **Transition** button on the toolbar) if you are in **Slide Sorter View**.

Slide Show

You can view the slide show as it would appear (projected onto a screen) by clicking on the **Slide Show** button (bottom of the screen).

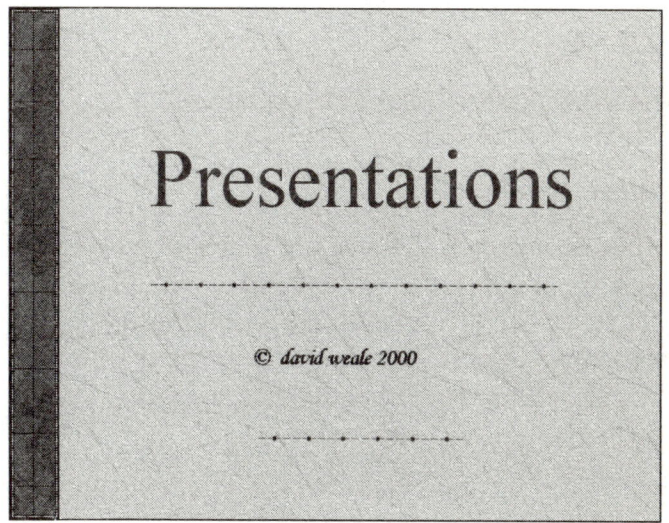

Using a projector is the most effective way of presenting and you can build in special effects such as **Transitions** and **Animations** (which you cannot do if you print the slides onto OHP film).

The Slide Show menu

If you click the right-hand mouse button during a slide show, the following menu is displayed.

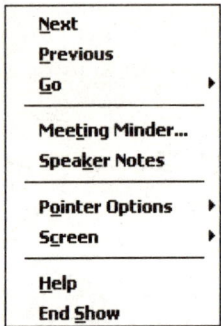

The most important of these are explained.

Next/Previous/Go

Use these commands to move to the next or previous point or slide.

The **Go** option has a sub menu.

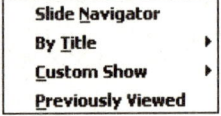

Slide Navigator/By Title

Selecting one of these displays a list of slides (**Navigator**) or titles (**Title**), if you choose one of these then the corresponding slide will be displayed. The **Navigator** menu is shown for reference.

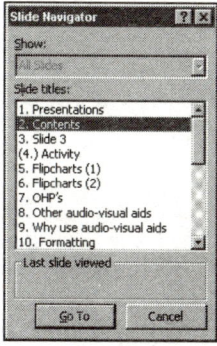

Custom Show

This jumps to a custom show (you have to have created a custom show - **Slide Show** and **Custom Shows**).

Meeting Minder

You can add notes or minutes during the presentation by selecting this option. Participants in an online meeting will all be able to see the notes.

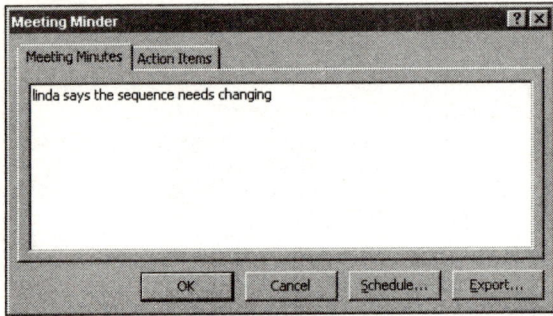

If you have **Word** or **Outlook** installed you can **Export** the text and action items (Word) or **Schedule** action items (Outlook).

Speaker Notes

If you have created speaker notes, these can be displayed on your screen during the presentation.

You can also add notes during the presentation.

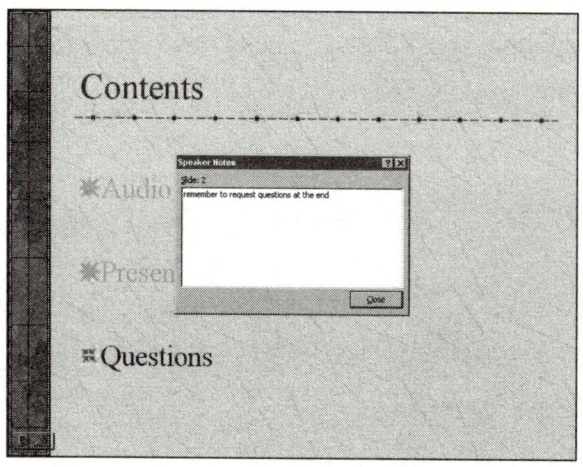

Pointer Options

You can change the arrow to a pen so that you can write on the screen (whether this is legible depends upon your mouse control).

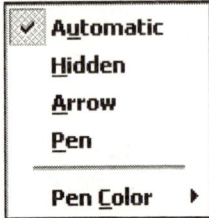

You can hide the pointer so that it never appears and you can alter the colour of the pen.

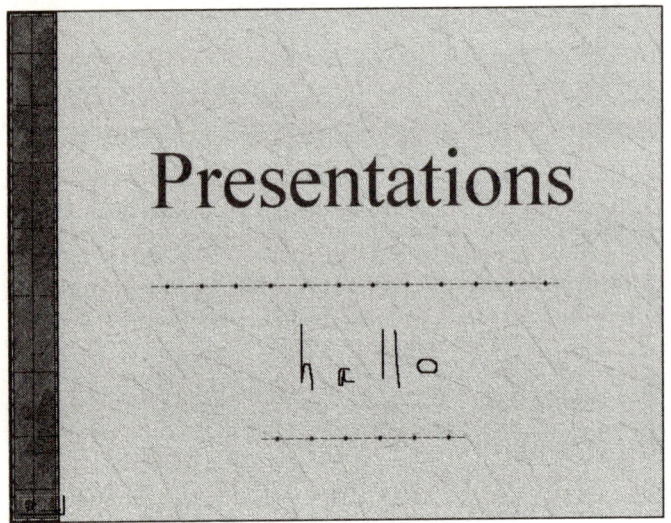

Screen/End Show

You can **Pause** the screen (when using automatic timings), **Black** the screen and if you have used the pen, you can **Erase** the pen (your writing).

```
Pause
Black Screen
Erase Pen
```

> I suggest you end the slide show either with a black screen or have a final slide that you can leave while you answer questions, for example your company logo. This is more professional than just ending the show and reverting to the program.

You can also choose to **End Show**, which ends it abruptly.

Printing

To print your file, click on the **Print** button on the upper toolbar, this prints to the default printer.

If you pull down the **File** menu and select **Print,** you will see the following dialogue box that offers you various choices.

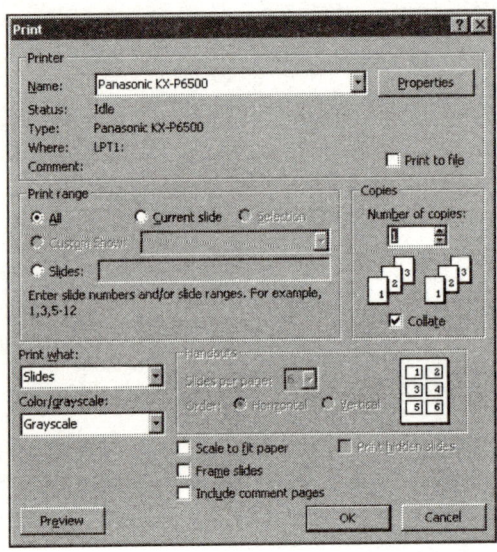

Print what

There is a choice of what to print.

Slides

This prints the individual slides, one to a page.

Handouts

Select **Handouts** (1, 2, 3, 4, 6 or 9 slides per page) to print off audience handouts, which give your audience both something to take away and something to annotate during the presentation.

Notes Pages

The slides and your notes are printed for each slide.

Outline View

Prints the outline view.

There are several printing options in the (bottom of) the dialogue box.

Scale to fit paper

Alters the scale to fit the paper size being used.

Frame slides

This prints a frame around each slide.

Include comment pages

Prints the comments you have added to individual slides (see section on comments).

Print hidden slides

You can hide slides within your presentation (so they do not appear when the slide show is run), if this option is selected, they would be included in the printout.

Saving Your Work

You should get into the habit of saving your work regularly so that any problems, whether hardware or software, do not cause too much loss of time or other problems. It is best to save to the **hard disc** as floppy discs are not as reliable.

To save your work you can click on the **Save** button on the toolbar along the top of the screen.

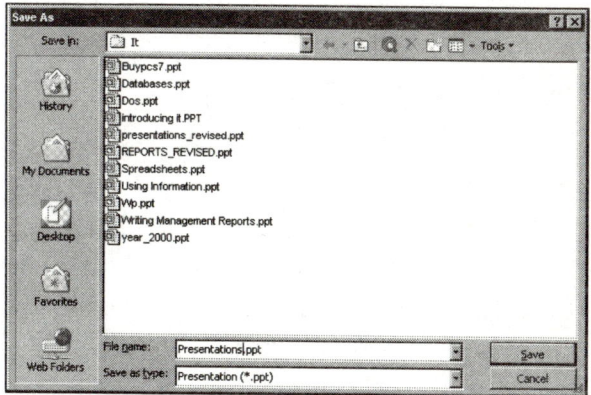

At this point, you can change where you save the file by clicking on the arrow to the right of **Save in** and alter the folder or disc you are saving to (use the buttons to locate the folder).

Next time if you use the **Save** button to save your work the process will be automatic and no dialogue box will appear.

> If you want to save to a different folder or filename then pull down the **File** menu and select **Save As**.

Note the **Save as type** option; you can save your file in a variety of different formats so that it can be opened in another program or an earlier version of the program (if you save it as an earlier version, some features that exist in PowerPoint 2002 may not be available).

> Any presentation created in Microsoft PowerPoint 95, PowerPoint 97, or PowerPoint 2000, can be opened in PowerPoint 2002.

Text

This section covers the various ways of entering and manipulating text within your presentation.

Entering Text

This is simple, click where prompted and begin typing.

When entering text use the return key to move on to the next point, a new bullet will appear below the original.

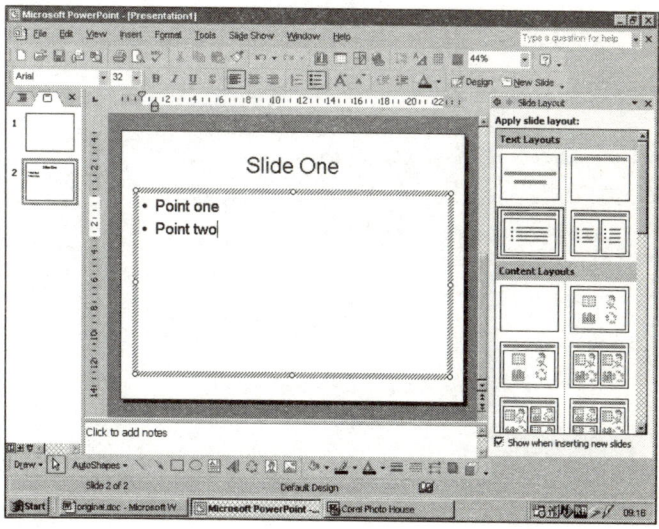

Altering the Font

Each design has fonts allocated to it, often these are ideal, but if you want to alter the fonts, there are several methods.

Highlight the text (by clicking and dragging the mouse to select the text), then click on the **Font** button along the upper toolbar and choose another font.

You can also alter the **Font Size** in the same way.

Alternatively, highlight the text, pull down the **Format** menu, and select **Font**, this gives more choices.

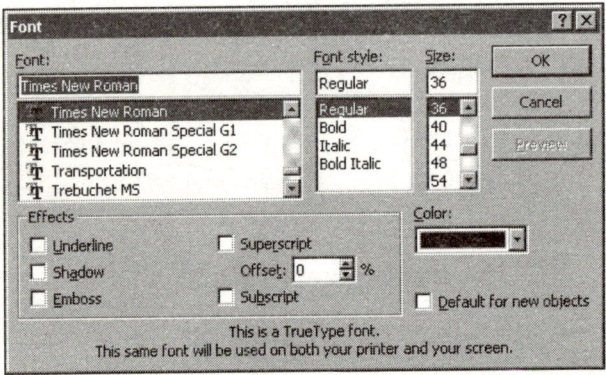

If you alter the **Master Slide**, the text within all the slides in the file changes to the new font/font size (see section on master slides).

Spell Checking Your Text

It is very easy to destroy the professionalism of your presentation by using incorrect spelling. Click the button along the upper toolbar and a dialogue box will appear.

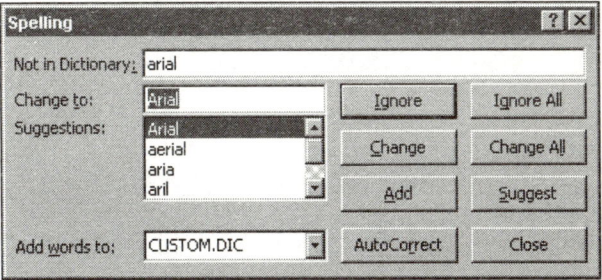

The way a spell checker operates is to compare every word you enter against a (finite) list of words.

If the word you type is not in the list, the spell checker program will identify it.

This does not mean it is wrong; merely that it is not in the dictionary.

You can **Add** words to your dictionary if you wish.

Graphics & Objects

It is useful and rewarding to add visuals to your presentation.

You can add:

- ClipArt (from the library that comes with the program)
- Pictures, sound and video clips
- Graphs
- WordArt
- Tables
- Organisation Charts
- Other objects

ClipArt

Choose the slide to which you want to add the image.

Click on the **Insert Clip Art** button on the **Drawing** toolbar (which should appear along the bottom of the screen, if it does not then pull down the **View** menu, select **Toolbars**, followed by **Drawing**).

The **Insert Clip Art** pane will appear on the right of the screen.

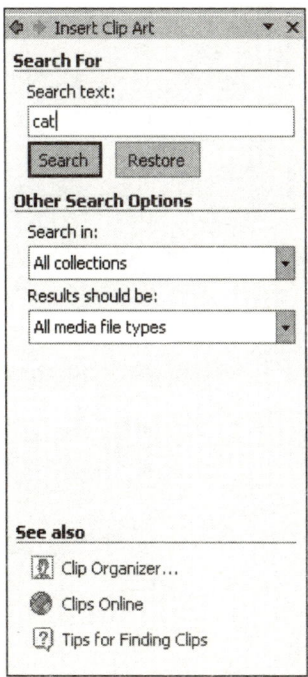

This can be used to search for relevant items by entering keywords in the **Search text** box and clicking the **Search** button.

The results are then shown (use the scrollbars to see all the items).

The **Modify** button enables the keyword search to be changed.

The image can be inserted directly into the presentation using **Insert**.

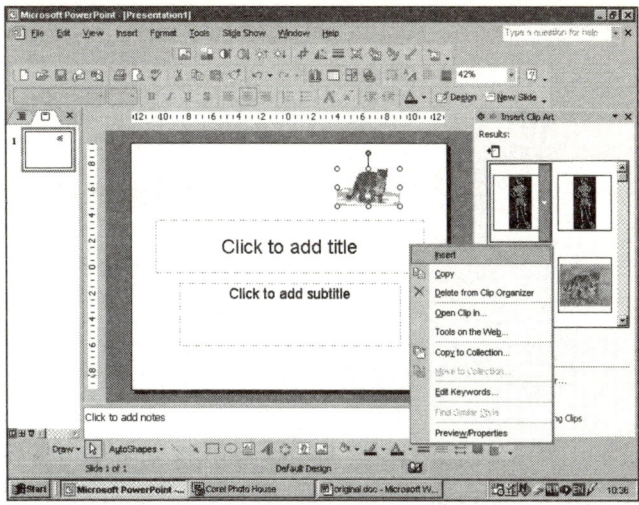

Alternatively, you can browse the collections of clip art by selecting the **Clip Organizer** option (at the bottom of the **Insert Clip Art** pane).

Select the category, e.g. **Office Collections** and then the image you want from the gallery.

Animated clip art items are shown with a small icon in the bottom right-hand corner of the illustration.

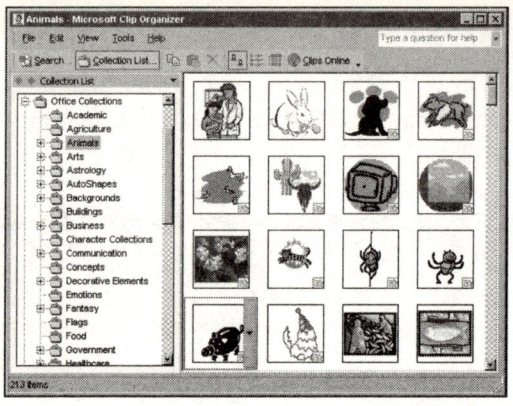

Click the arrow to the right of the item; this will display a menu from which you select, e.g. **Copy** or **Insert**.

Pictures, sounds and videos

Photographs, sounds and motion (video) clips can be added to your slide show and are included within the gallery.

To search for specific types of media (e.g. sounds), click the **Results should be: (Insert Clip** Art pane) and ensure only those media types are clicked.

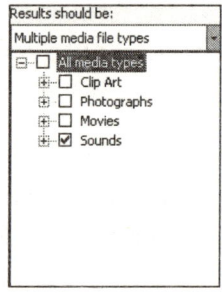

Graphs

You can create and insert graphs by clicking on the toolbar button.

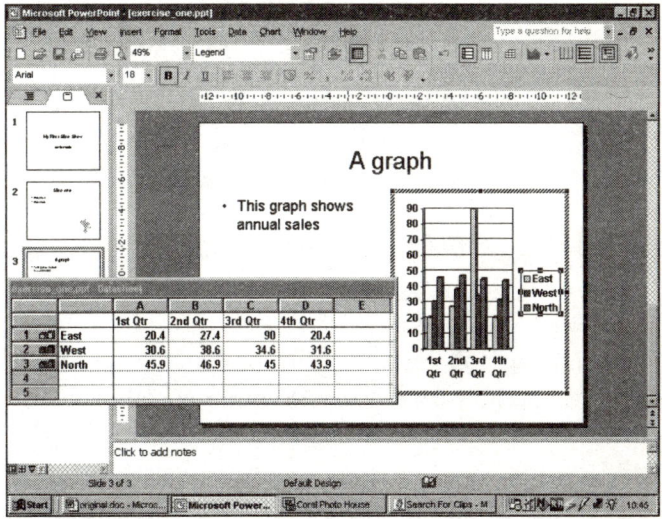

This loads **Microsoft Graph** (an application that can be accessed from all the main applications, e.g. **PowerPoint** or **Word**).

You create your own graph by altering and/or adding to the data shown.

When the chart is selected, some new buttons appear on the toolbar (the **View Datasheet** button is only visible if you show the toolbar buttons on two rows).

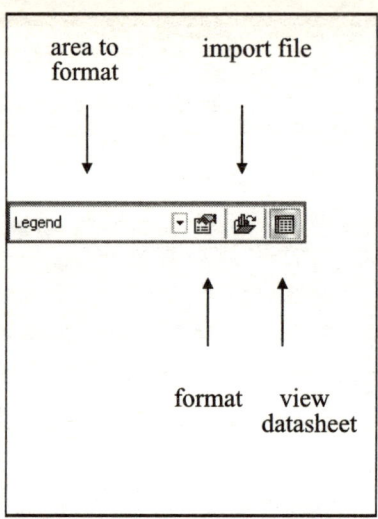

You alter the graph by using the buttons. Graphs can be sized and so on in a similar way to other visuals.

To alter a graph, double-click it and you can then edit it as you wish by using the various features of the **Graph** application.

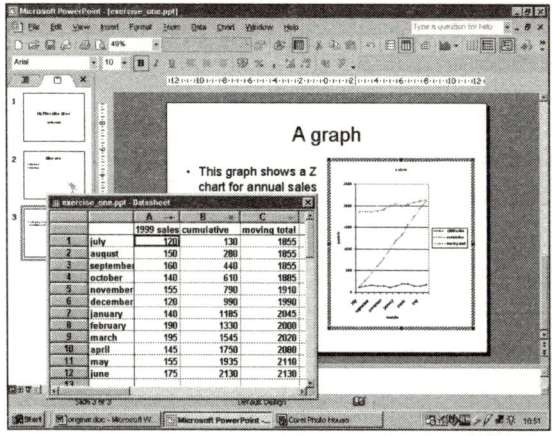

You can import data from a spreadsheet program such as **Excel** or insert an existing graph from **Excel** by using the **Insert (Object)** pull-down menu (or **Paste** a graph from the originating program).

Here is a **Z chart** I imported from an **Excel** workbook.

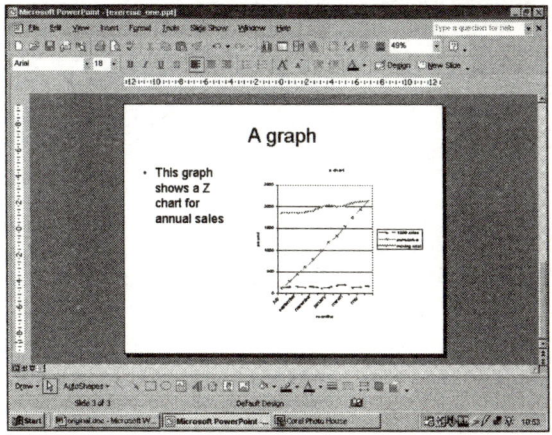

WordArt

Another object you can insert into your presentation is **WordArt**. You can use this to create special text effects and fancy lettering for logos or titles.

Click the **Insert WordArt** button (**Drawing** toolbar) to begin the process; you will see the following screen.

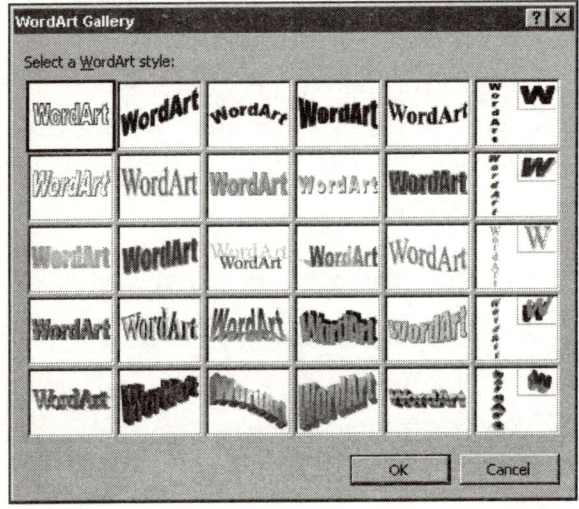

Select the style you want (you can change it later) and click **OK**, the screen will show a text entry box.

Enter your text in the box (returning to create a new line) and then use the buttons to create the effect you want.

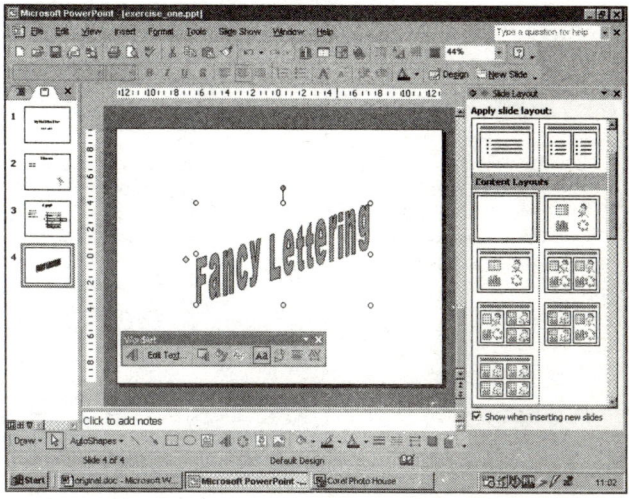

The text can be altered using the **WordArt** toolbar.

To alter your **WordArt** object double-click it and **WordArt** will be loaded again.

Tables

Tables are very useful to lay out text or images in columns.

Creating tables within PowerPoint

Insert a new slide, choosing the tables layout (as shown in the illustration) from the **Slide Layout** pane.

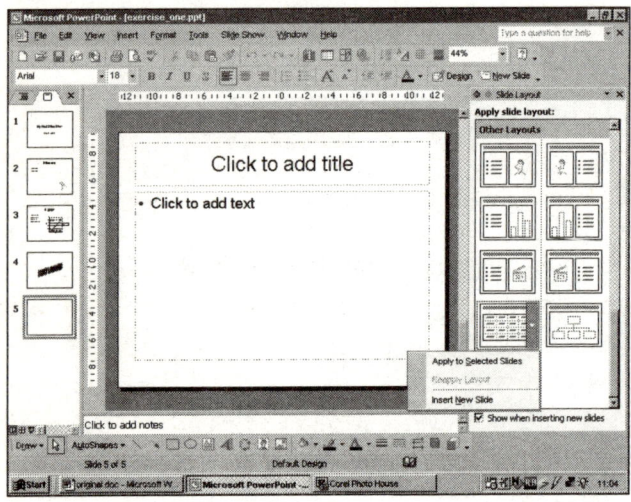

You will then see the following screen.

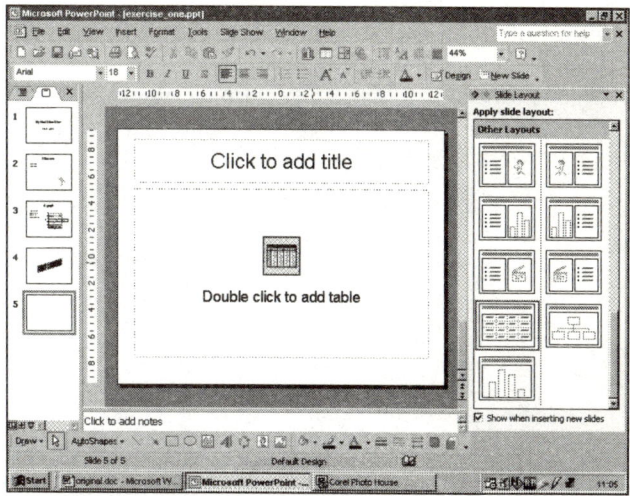

Double-click the image and decide how many rows and columns you want (you can add or delete them at a later stage if necessary).

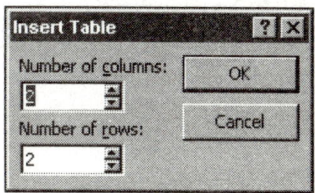

Another method is to pull down the **Insert** menu and select **Table**, this will insert a table into an existing slide.

Alternatively, click the **Table** button, this lets you highlight the number of rows and columns you want in your table.

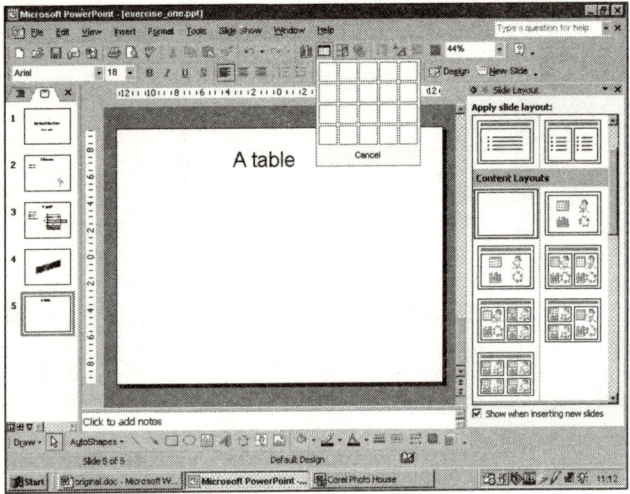

Whichever method is used, a table will appear, along with the **Tables** toolbar (as shown in the illustration).

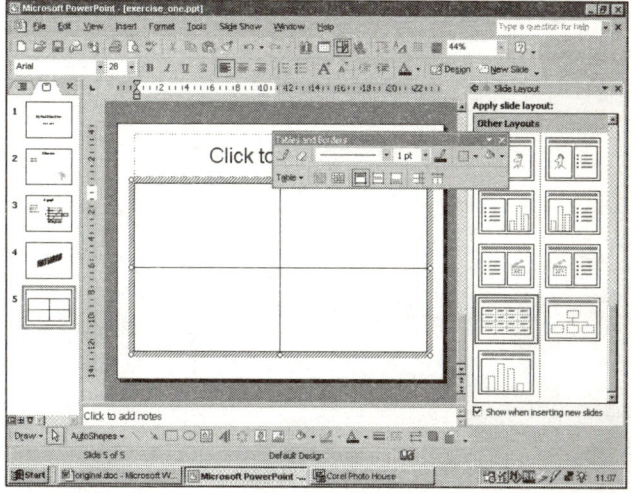

You can use the toolbar buttons to create the effects you want; here is an example.

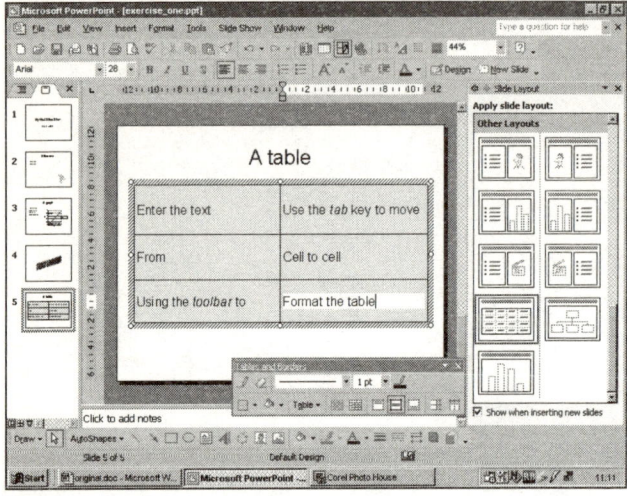

Sometimes it may be preferable to create a table in **Word** and then **Paste** it into **PowerPoint** as **Word** contains very powerful table features.

Organisation Charts

One of the advantages of a program such as **PowerPoint** is the variety of predesigned diagrams and other graphics available.

To insert an organisation chart into your presentation, use the organisation chart slide layout (**Slide Layout** pane).

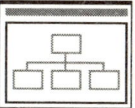

After selecting this, you will see the slide, double-click the symbol and you can begin to create your organisation chart.

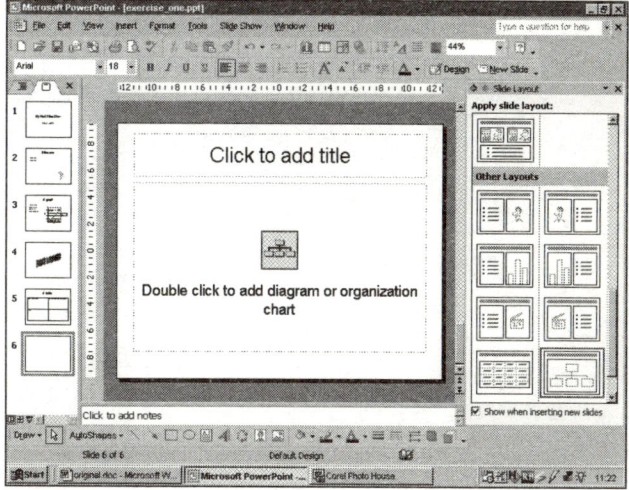

There is a choice of charts, which are described in the **Diagram Gallery** that then appears.

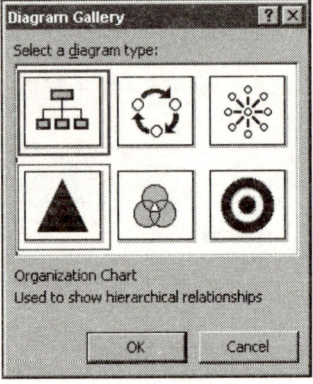

Select the first of these and the **Microsoft Organization Chart** module will appear.

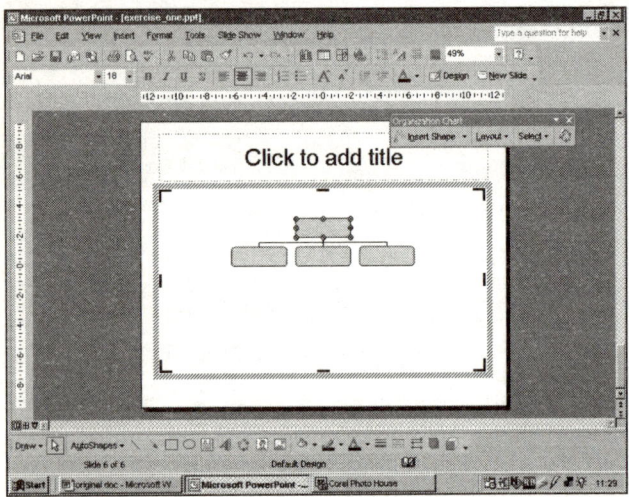

You enter the names and titles by clicking the relevant box and typing, you can add or delete the boxes.

Here is an example of a competed organisation chart.

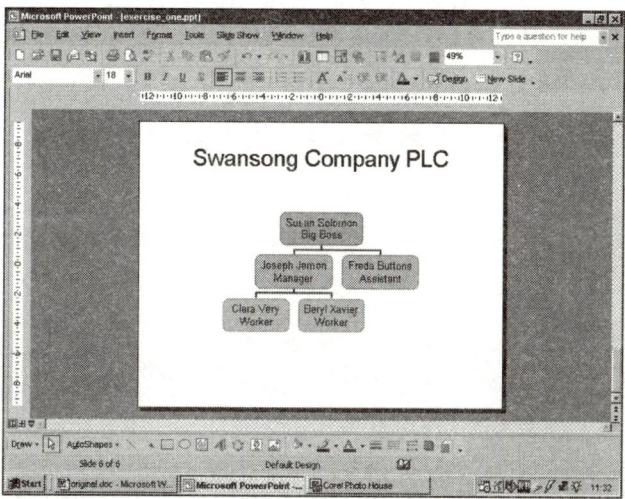

The commands specific to the organisation chart are described briefly below.

Organization Chart Toolbar

The toolbar extends the functionality of the chart, note the (down) arrow on the title bar, this enables you to **Add or Remove Buttons** from the toolbar or to **Customize** the contents (all toolbars allow customisation in this way).

Insert Shape

Use **Insert Shape** to add boxes to the chart by selecting a box and then clicking **Insert Shape.**

Clicking the down arrow to the right of the **Insert Shape** button displays the choices.

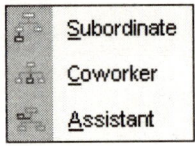

Layout

Clicking the arrow on the button displays the variety of layout formatting tools to apply to the organisation chart.

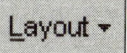

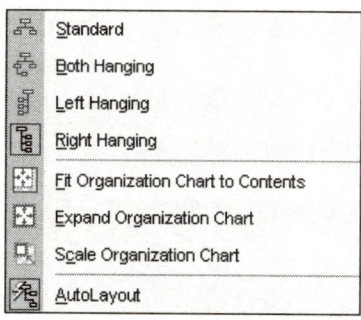

Select

The **Select** button enables you to select all or part of the chart (you can also click and drag the mouse to achieve the same effect).

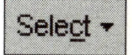

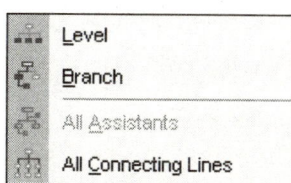

AutoFormat

This is a quick and easy way to apply formatting to the chart.

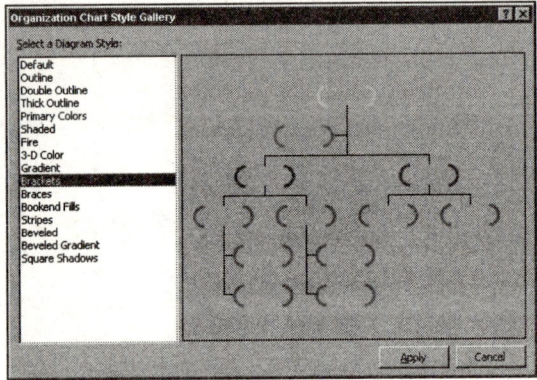

Choose the effect you want and it will be imposed onto the chart.

Other Objects

There are several other objects you can add to your presentation, e.g. **Microsoft Equation 3** (using this you can enter very complex mathematical symbols and equations).

To access these, pull down the **Insert** menu, followed by **Object** and select from the list.

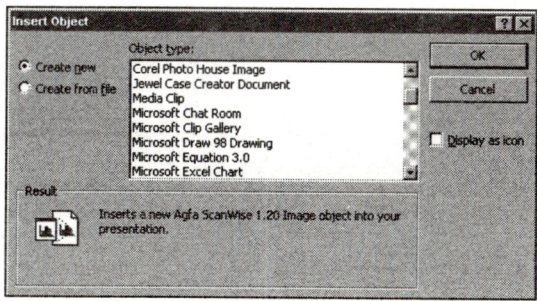

Artwork

Manipulating Images

There are various techniques to manipulate (most) images.

Moving an Image (or Other Object)

Make sure that the image has been selected, then click the mouse within the image (it becomes a four-headed cross) and while holding down the mouse button move the image to a new position.

Sizing an Image

There are two ways to achieve this.

- Select the image and then position the mouse pointer on one of the corners of the image. The mouse pointer should become a small line with arrows at either end. While keeping the mouse button held down, move the mouse in or out to resize the image.
- Alternatively, click the image, pull down the **Format** menu, and select **Picture** (**Object** or **WordArt**). You will see a dialogue box; all you need to do is to enter the percentage you want to scale to (right-clicking the object and selecting **Format** from the displayed list may be quicker).

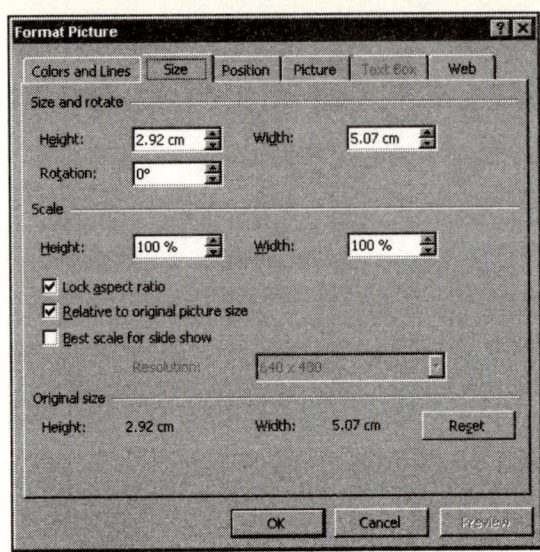

Alternatively, use the **Picture** toolbar buttons (if the toolbar is not displayed when you click the image, pull down the **View** menu and select **Toolbars**).

Cropping an Object

Cropping is different from sizing. Sizing makes the whole image smaller (or bigger), but when you crop an object, you remove part of the whole object from view.

This is sometimes useful to remove extraneous parts of a picture or other image.

To do this, display the **Picture** toolbar and the cropping tool will be shown (the toolbar may appear automatically when you select the image, if it does not, pull down the **View** menu, selecting **Toolbars**).

You then grab any corner or side of your object with the tool and remove part of the object.

You can bring back any part of a cropped image in the same way you removed it, as it is only removed from view, not actually deleted.

Customising Slides

This section deals with the methods of customising your presentation so that it stands out from other presentations.

The Master Slide

You can make changes to all the slides by amending the **Master** slide.

To do this, pull down the **View** menu and select **Master**. You choose which type of master to alter from the list shown below.

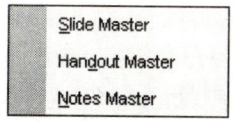

You will then see the **Master** appear and any changes or additions you make to this will be reflected in all the slides of that style (i.e. if you have changed the **Slide Master** this will not affect the **Title** slide).

Below is an example of a **Slide Master** with the fonts changed and made larger. Any slides within that file should take on these new attributes (although this may not happen to *previously* created slide shows that have been customised).

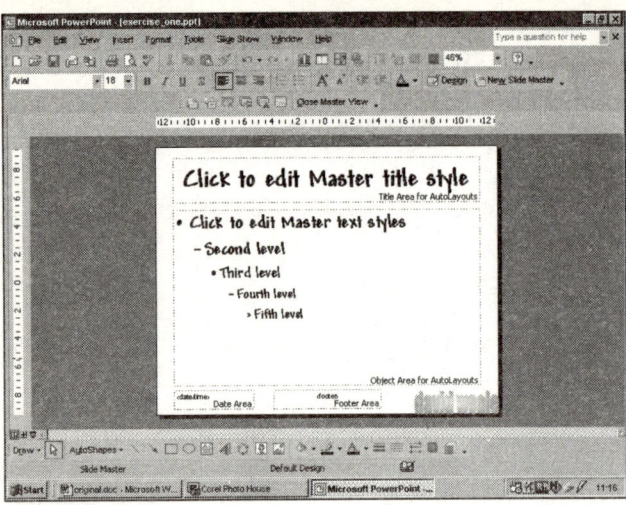

It is best to create your master slide layout (including transitions, animations, etc.) before creating the slide show, as your choices will affect the number of lines and number of characters on each line.

Deleting Slides

There are two ways to achieve this:

In **Normal View** pull down the **Edit** menu and then select **Delete Slide**.

In **Slide Sorter View** select the slide or slides by clicking on them and press the **Delete** key.

You can select multiple slides using the **Shift** or **CTRL** keys while you click the slides.

Clicking the initial slide and then holding down the **Shift** key while clicking the last slide (you want to select) will select all the slides, using the **Ctrl** key allows non-sequential slides to be selected.

Drawing toolbar

If you are doing any work with graphics, then you will want to display the **Drawing** toolbar. I work with it permanently displayed.

To display any toolbar, pull down the **View** menu and select **Toolbars**. Click on your choice. The toolbar will be displayed.

There are some very useful tools here, for example, you can add **text boxes** and **arrows** to any part of your slides.

Draw

If you click on this, a further menu is displayed.

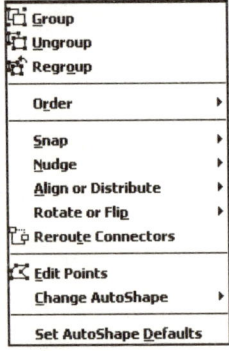

Grouping and Ungrouping

You may want to use only a part of an image or you may want to rearrange it.

Ungrouping breaks up the image into its component parts.

It is not possible to ungroup certain types of image.

To ungroup an image, select it and then choose **Ungroup**.

A message may appear on the screen, which you can agree to (if you want to ungroup the image).

You will see that the image is now made up of many sub-images all with little squares surrounding them.

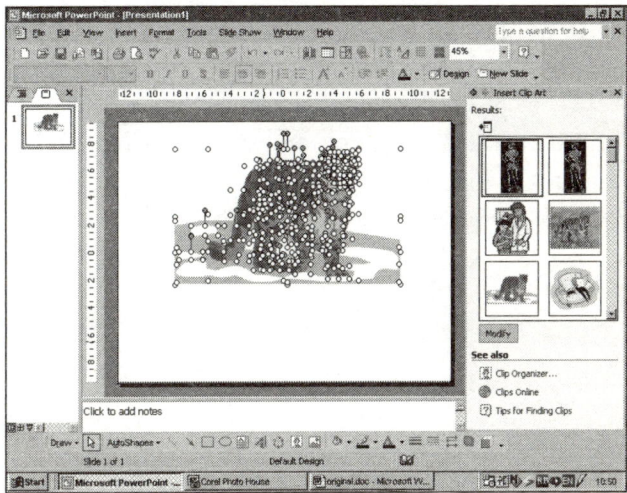

Click outside the image and then click on any sub-image and you can move it, colour it, size it or delete it as you wish (it may also be possible to ungroup a sub-image).

To select more than one component or object, hold down the **Shift** key while clicking the mouse on each item you want to select.

Merging images

You can join several images into one so that they form a single group, which can then be moved or resized, you can do this in several ways.

☐ Hold down the mouse button and drag the mouse around the items. This will select all the items.

☐ While holding down the **Shift** key, click the mouse on each item you want to include within the group.

☐ Pull down the **Edit** menu and choose **Select All**. Then (whichever method is used) choose **Group** or **Regroup** from the **Draw** menu to combine all the images.

Superimposing One Image on Another

A useful technique is to use two or more images to create a new one.

Insert the two images and carry out any manipulation and then select both and group them (so they form one image, which can then be manipulated).

Below is an example of two images used together, the original one was ungrouped, one part deleted and the components rearranged. The second image, the donkey, was sized and then moved onto the blackboard.

Order

If you place one object on top of another, the order in which these can be displayed can be critical to the result.

Think of the objects as being stacked, one on top of the next.

The commands to vary the sequence are:

Bring to Front

This brings the selected object to the top of the pile.

Send to Back

This sends the selected object to the bottom of the pile.

Bring Forward

This brings the selected object forward one level in the pile.

Send Backward

This sends the selected object back one level in the pile.

Grid and Guides

There is an (invisible) grid and any object or text aligns itself to this. It makes lining up easier to achieve but does reduce fine control.

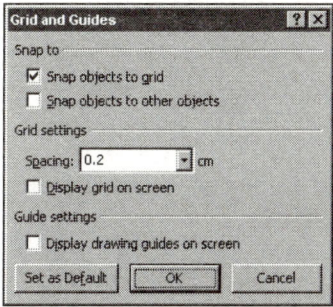

The dialogue box can be used to display the gridlines (or guides).

Nudge

If you have selected an object, you can nudge it in various directions.

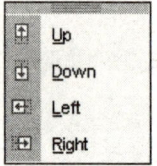

Align or Distribute

This is used to align objects and/or text, you have to select more than one object or text for this to be usable, and then simply pull down the **Draw** menu and **Align or Distribute**.

You have a choice of alignments and you can experiment with this technique.

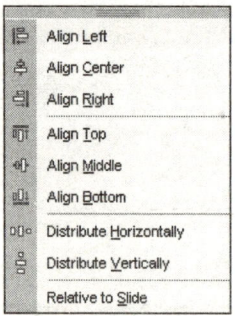

Save the file before making any experimental changes to it.

Rotate or Flip

You can rotate or flip (selected) objects within **PowerPoint**.

To do so, select the **Draw** menu and select **Rotate or Flip**. You will be given the following choices.

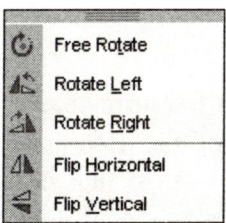

Free Rotate lets you grab any of the corners with the rotate tool and rotate to your heart's desire. Below is an example (the donkey has been flipped).

If your image will not allow you to choose **Rotate or Flip** then you may be able to **Ungroup** it (**Draw** menu) and then **Group** it again, it becomes a **PowerPoint** object and can be rotated.

Rotating Text

As well as being able to rotate objects, **PowerPoint** enables you to rotate text.

To do this simply select the text and use the **Drawing** toolbar, select **Draw** and then **Rotate or Flip**.

Edit Points

If you have created a freeform shape (e.g. by using any of the freeform tools (shown opposite) in the **AutoShapes Lines**), you can then move or edit the points within that object.

Change AutoShape

If you have created an **AutoShape**, and you select this option (while the **AutoShape** object is still selected) then you can choose another shape and the original shape will be converted into the new one.

AutoShapes

The AutoShapes menu is shown below.

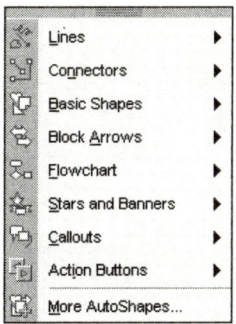

Each of these displays **AutoShapes**. The **Flowchart** shapes are shown for reference.

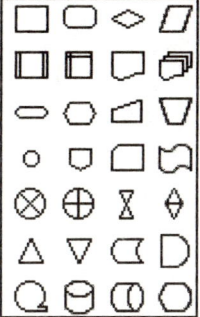

You select the symbol you want and then click and drag to produce the shape.

Once you have done this, you can manipulate the image as you wish, e.g. alter the shape, the colour and so on.

PowerPoint and the Web

With the growing importance and use of the Internet, the **Microsoft Office** programs are increasingly containing web tools.

These tools enable files to be converted into a format that can be used on the Internet or company Intranets without very much work or the need for extensive knowledge of HTML coding.

Saving a presentation as HTML

The simplest method is to save your file as a web page.

To do so pull down the **File** menu and select **Save as Web Page**.

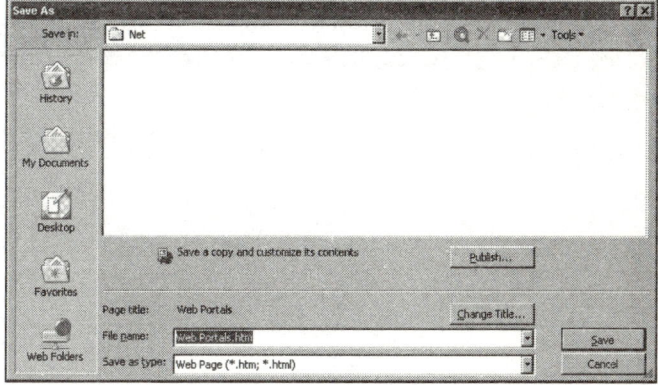

This saves the existing file as a web page (with an .HTM extension) and if you open it, you will see a screen similar to this.

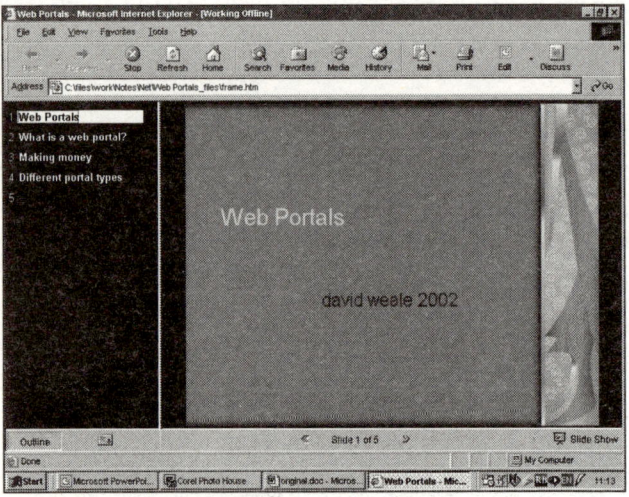

You can click the slide names (on the left of the screen) to see each individual slide or if you click the **Slide Show** button on the (bottom) right, the slide show will be run.

Alternatively, after selecting **Save as Web Page** from the **File** menu, you can click the **Publish** button, which allows you to customise the contents.

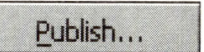

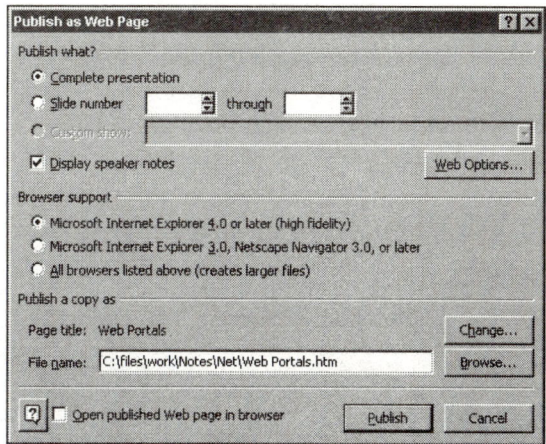

When you want to publish the pages to your web server, you need to enter the address for this in the **File name** section.

Note the option at the bottom, if you tick this then the browser will be loaded and the pages displayed without any further intervention on your part.

You can also see how your pages will look (as web pages) by using the **File** menu and then **Web Page Preview**.

Web file structure

When you save the **PowerPoint** file as web pages, what is created are an index page and a folder containing a file for each of the pages within the presentation.

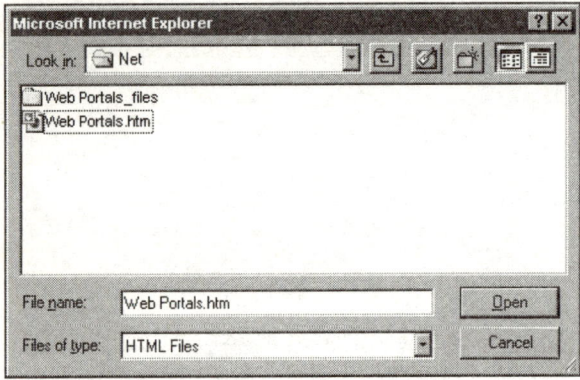

Adding hyperlinks

You can add a hyperlink to a slide, either as an **Action Button** (explained later) or as a normal hyperlink.

To do this, highlight the text or select an object and click the **Hyperlink** button on the toolbar. Then enter the necessary data into the dialogue box.

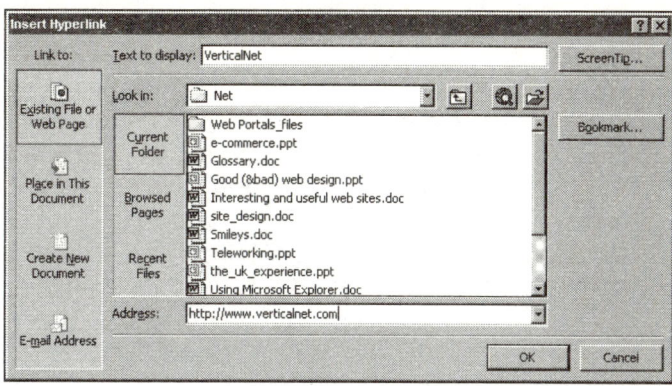

You can then click the hyperlink and go to the file or web page identified in the link when you run the actual slide show (e.g. in this example **VerticalNet**).

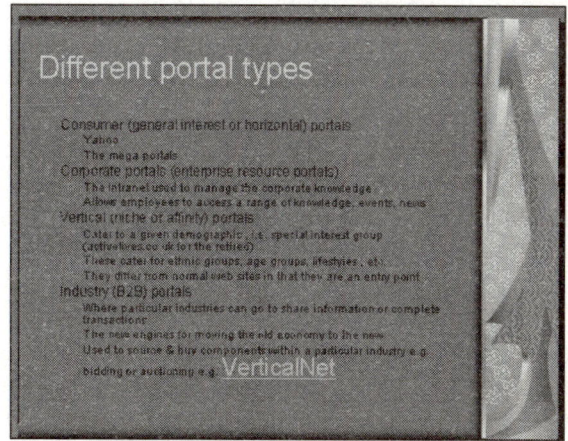

The Pull Down Menus

In this section of the book, I have covered the commands in the pull-down menus that have not been dealt with previously.

You may see an arrow at the bottom of the pull-down menus; this means that there are additional commands, which you access by clicking the arrow.

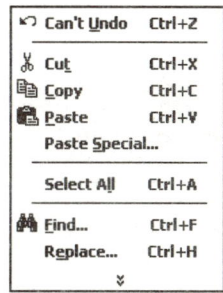

You can also set the full menus to appear as the default by using the **Tools** menu, followed by **Customize** and **Options** and ticking the **Always show full menus** box.

File menu

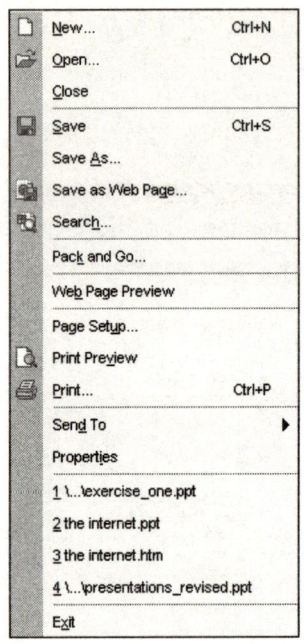

Search

A new feature, this enables a search for files containing specified text. The search can be narrowed using **Other Search Options** and there is an **Advanced Search** available (bottom of pane).

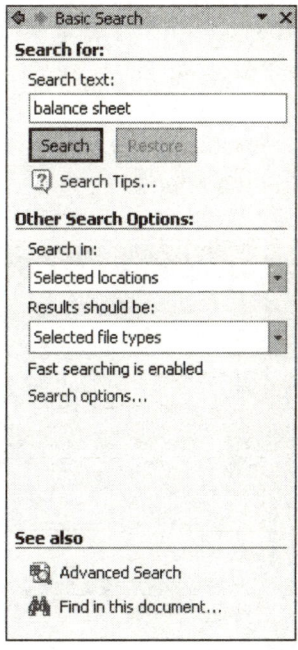

The search results in a list of files, any of which can be opened by clicking the filename.

Pack and Go

You can save a presentation on a floppy disc so that it can be used on any computer whether it has **PowerPoint** installed or not.

If you have used fonts in your presentation which may not be present on the host computer, then you can embed them into the presentation.

You can also incorporate the viewer if the host computer does not have a copy installed.

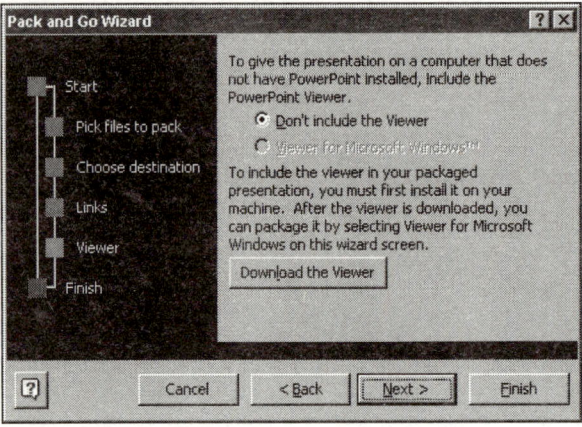

You will be prompted for additional discs if the files do not fit onto a single disc.

Web Page Preview

This displays the slides as they appear within a web browser.

Page Setup

The default is on-screen shows, however this be varied if desired using this dialogue box.

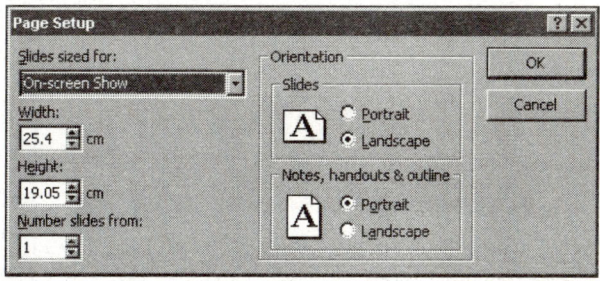

Print Preview

A new feature for **PowerPoint**, this lets you preview the way the presentations will look when printed (whether slides, handouts or notes pages).

The preview can be changed by pulling down the **Print What** list (located on the toolbar at the top of the screen).

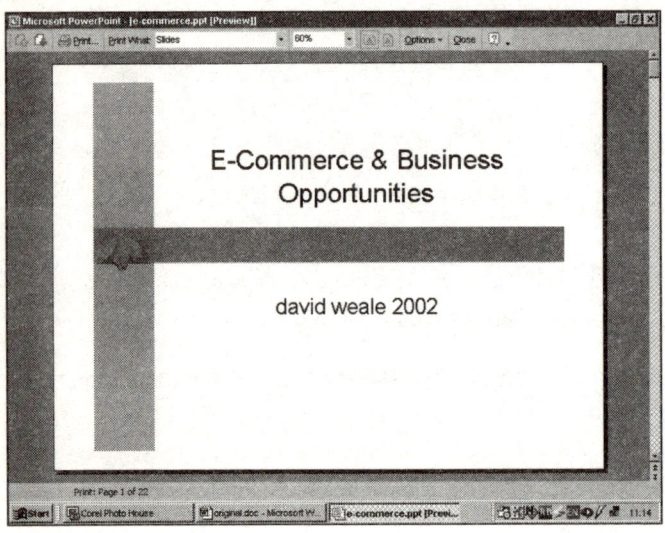

Send To

You can send a file to various places, e.g. to an e-mail address for review or as an attachment.

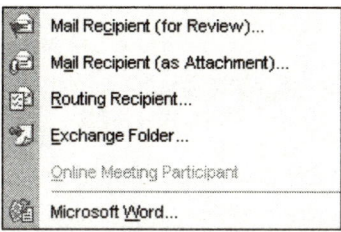

Mail Recipient

You can send the file via e-mail.

The e-mail program is loaded and the file automatically included as an attachment.

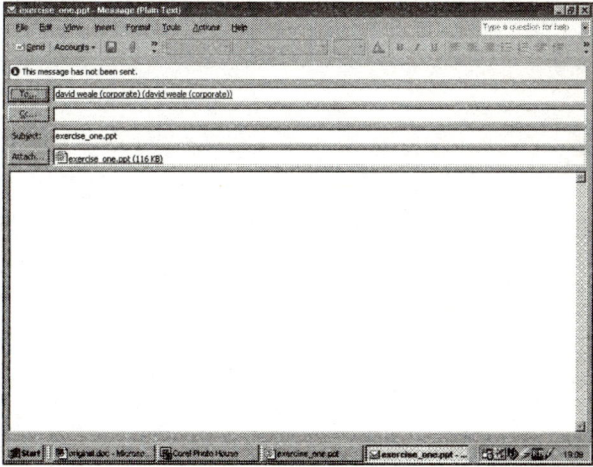

Routing Recipient

If you want the recipients to look at your file one at a time and (perhaps) add comments, then you can route the presentation to one recipient after another and each will see the previous comments.

You can track the progress of the file and when it has been to all the recipients, it will automatically be returned to you.

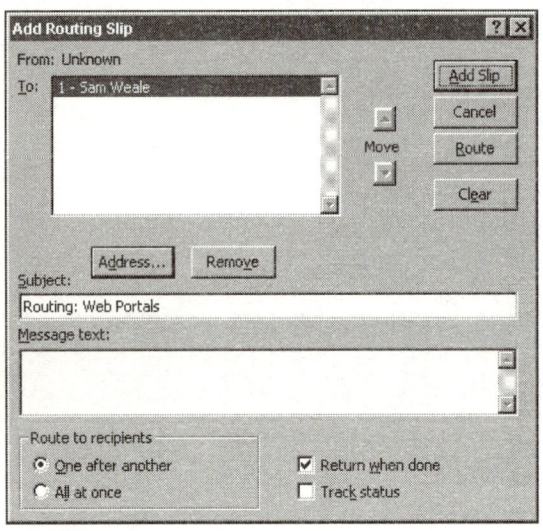

Exchange Folder

You can post the file to a **Microsoft Exchange** public folder, so that anyone with access to the folder can look at the file.

Microsoft Word

You can send the file to **Word**. The dialogue box gives you various choices about how the slides will appear within the Word document.

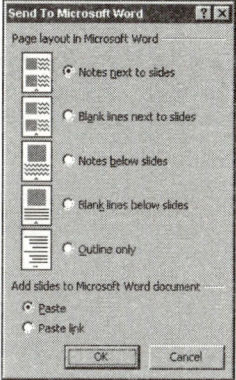

The results may look like this, depending upon the choices you made within the dialogue box.

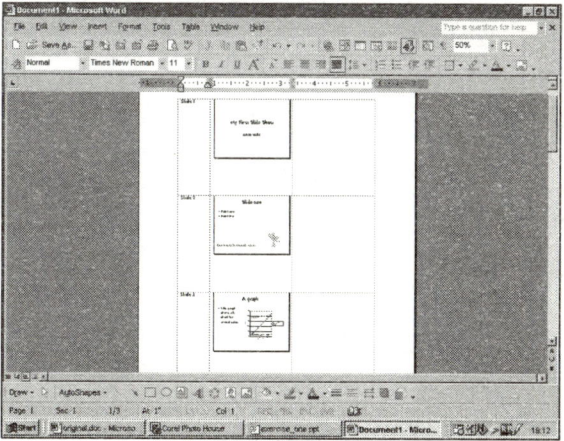

Properties

This displays screens of information about the file (some of which can be altered).

The **Statistics** screen is shown for reference.

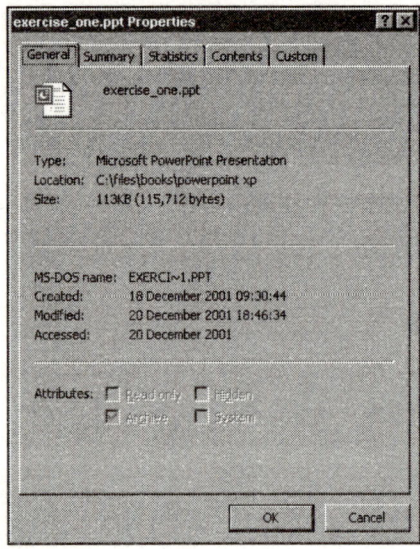

Edit menu

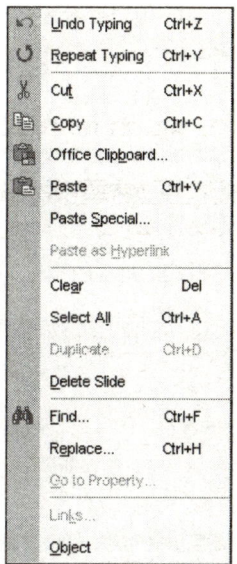

Cut, Copy and Paste

Text or images can be **Cut**, **Copy** or **Paste**(d), using the appropriate buttons on the toolbar.

Office Clipboard

By pulling down the **Edit** menu, followed by **Office Clipboard**, the contents of the clipboard will be displayed in the **Task** pane (on the right of the screen).

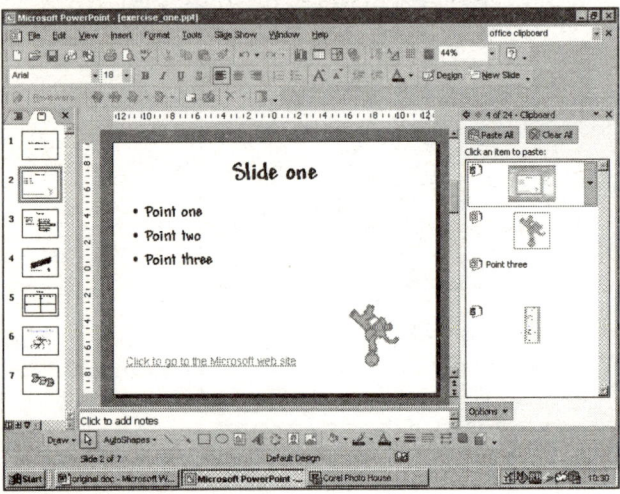

By selecting any item, you can **Paste** it into the current slide (or by clicking the arrow on the side, **Delete** or **Paste** the item into the current slide).

Paste Special

This is similar to the **Paste** command but gives you more control over the format and allows you to create a link to the original application.

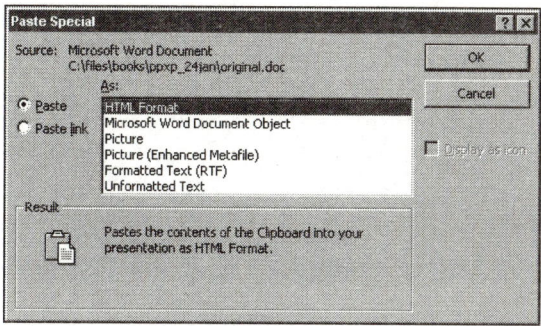

If an object is linked, it will be automatically updated whenever the original is changed.

Paste as Hyperlink

You can copy and paste text or objects as hyperlinks.

For example, you may want to paste another slide title (into the present slide) as a hyperlink to that slide, so that if the viewer clicks on the hyperlink then they can jump to that slide.

You can also link to web sites by highlighting text (or selecting an image) and clicking the **Insert Hyperlink** button.

Clear

Selecting this will clear (delete) the selected object or highlighted text.

Select All

This selects all the items (text and objects) on a particular slide or if in **Slide Sorter View** will select all the slides.

Duplicate

This allows you to duplicate a slide so that an identical copy is added to the presentation (next to the original). Select the required slide, then pull down the **Edit** menu, and click on **Duplicate** (it only works in **Slide Sorter View** or if you have selected an item within the slide).

Delete Slide

By pulling down the **Edit** menu and choosing **Delete Slide**, you can delete the current slide (or the selected slide(s) in **Slide Sorter View**).

You can also delete a slide in **Slide Sorter View** by selecting the slide(s) and then pressing the **Del** key.

You can use the **Undo** button if you quickly realise you have deleted the slide(s) accidentally.

Find

A standard text tool, this enables you to find words or parts of words within your presentation.

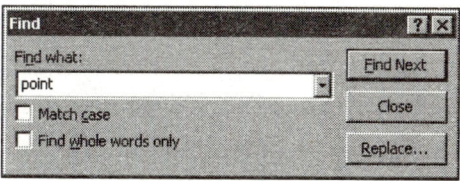

You enter the word or phrase you are looking for and click on the **Match case** and/or **Find whole words only**, if this is what you wish.

Click on the **Find Next** button and the first occurrence of the word will be found. Then you can move to the next by clicking on the **Find Next** button and so on.

> You can also use **Shift** and **F4** to repeat the search.

Replace

This replaces the word or phrase with another.

Go to Property

If you set custom properties (**File**, **Properties**) then you can go to the property within the slide using this option.

Links

If you select this option, you will see a dialogue box displayed that lets you alter the links.

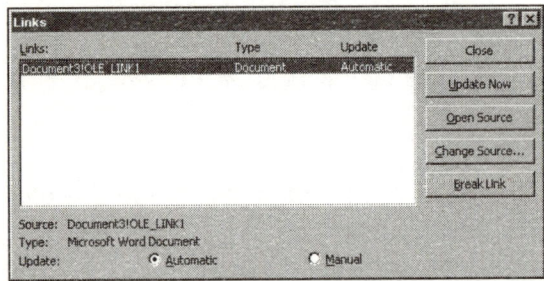

This option is not available until you have selected a linked object within your presentation, e.g. a link created using **Paste Link**.

Objects/Text

You can edit objects/text by selecting the item and pulling down the **Edit** menu followed by **Objects** (or more quickly by double clicking the mouse on the object).

View menu

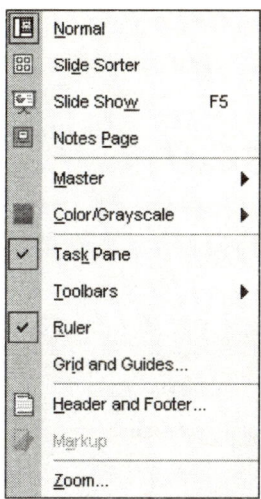

Color/Grayscale

This enables the slides to be viewed in greyscale, colour or black and white.

Toolbars

You can add or remove any toolbars.

To do this, pull down the **View** menu and select **Toolbars**. You will see the dialogue box (shown below).

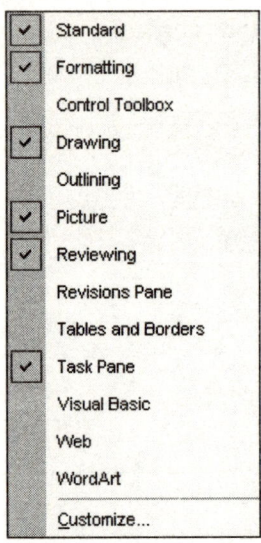

By selecting or deselecting the different toolbars you can add (or remove) them.

You can move a toolbar on the screen by moving the mouse pointer to the beginning of the toolbar (the cursor becomes a double-headed cross) and then dragging it to a new position.

Once a toolbar is selected, you can change the shape by moving the mouse pointer along an edge until it becomes a two-headed arrow that can then be dragged to produce a new shape.

Rulers

You can display the vertical and horizontal rulers by selecting this option.

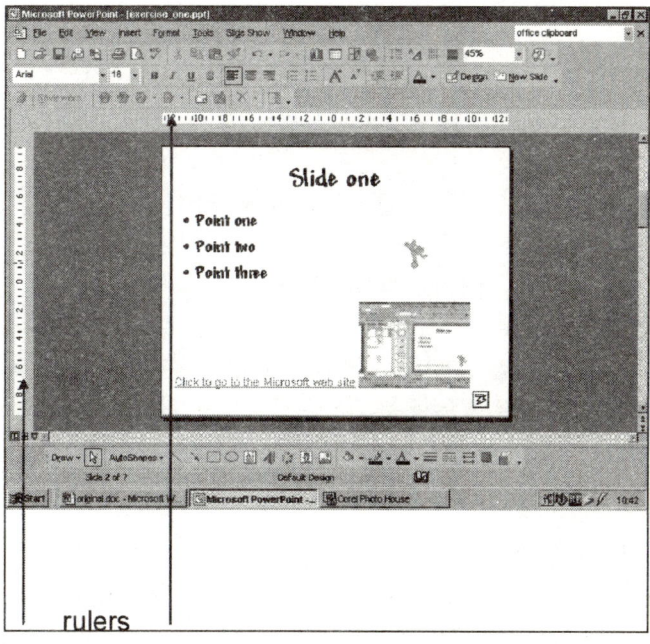
rulers

Grid and Guides

You can display or hide the guides by using the **View** menu and then **Grid and Guides**.

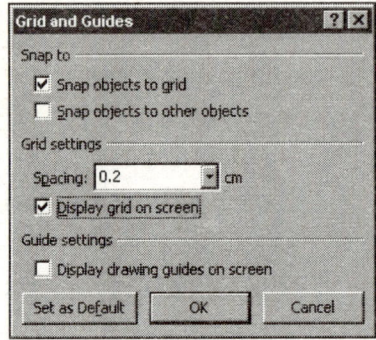

Guides are useful to position objects or text and they can be moved horizontally or vertically by clicking the mouse pointer on the guide and dragging it.

You can display them on screen by selecting the option **Display grid on screen**.

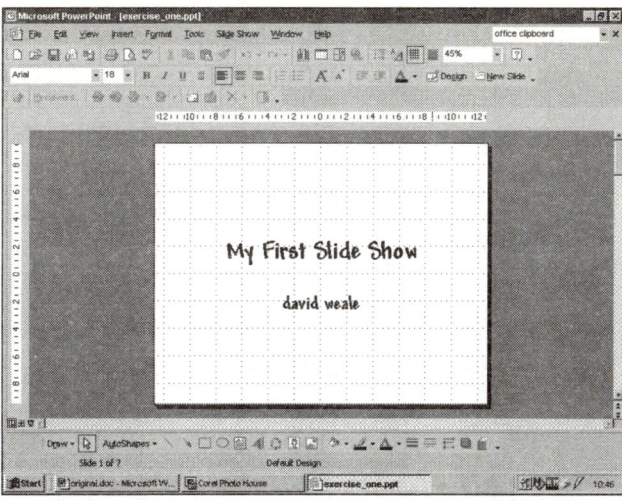

Header and Footer

You can insert the date and time, slide numbers and footers (you type in the text) using this.

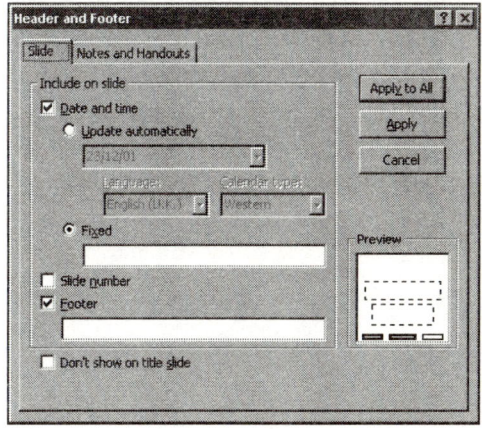

The **Notes and Handouts** option lets you do the same for the notes and handout pages (headers are unavailable on slides but are enabled on notes and handouts).

You can see how footers appear from the illustration.

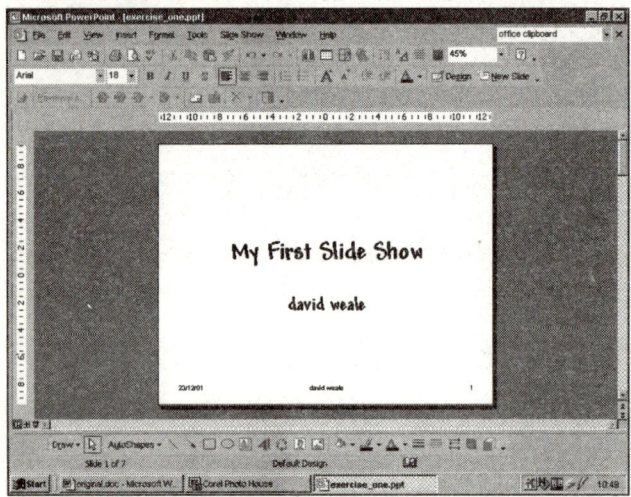

Markup

This displays any comments you have added to the slide (or hides the comments).

You need to have inserted the comments (**Insert** followed by **Comments**) as you can see in the upper left of the illustration.

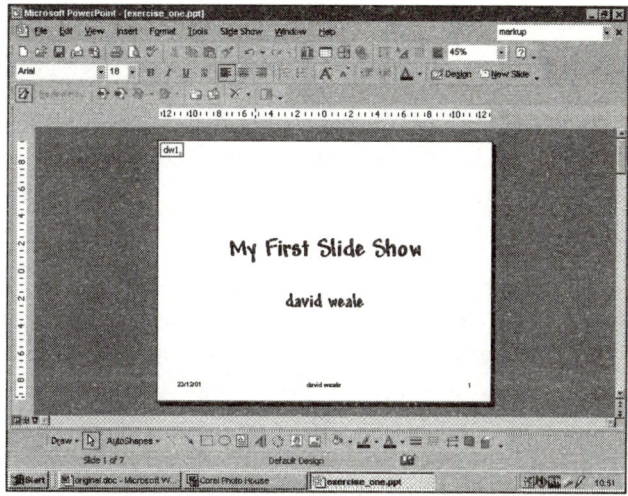

Insert menu

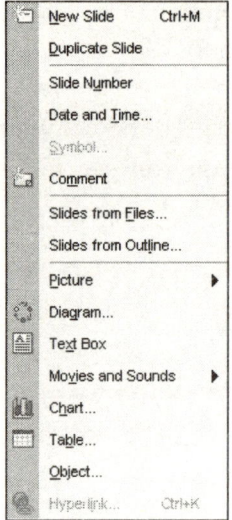

Duplicate Slide

This creates a copy of the current slide and inserts it into the slide show. Useful if you are only making minor alterations to a slide.

Slide Number / Date and Time

Normally you would use the **Header and Footer** command (**View** menu) to insert page numbers and dates on the **Master** or on individual slides, however this is an alternative.

Symbol

You can insert symbols from a variety of character sets into a **text box** within a slide.

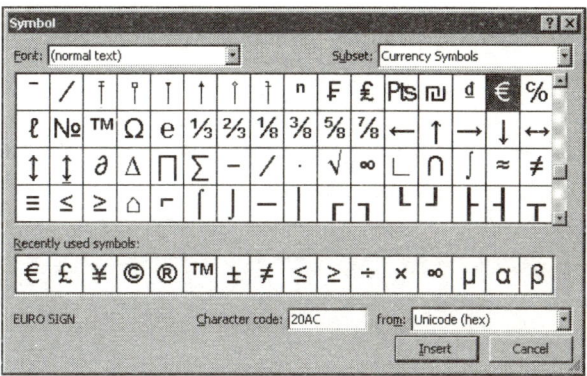

Comment

You can insert comments onto your slides; simply select this option and type in the comment you want to make. You can hide or display the comments by using the **View** menu and clicking **Comments**.

The comments are for your information; they do not appear when you run the **Slide Show** or print out **Handouts**.

Slides from Files

This option lets you add slides from another file into your current presentation.

To do this, pull down the **Insert** menu and select **Slides from Files**.

You will see a dialogue box and you select the file and then click the slides you want to add.

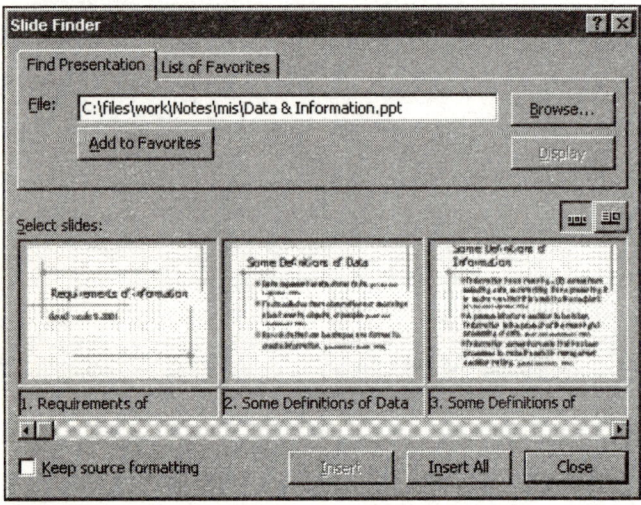

The new slides will be added after the current slide, and the other slides will be re-sequenced.

You may find it easiest to use **Slide Sorter View** and position the cursor where you want the new slides to be added.

Slides from Outline

This is slightly different in that **PowerPoint** will automatically create a slide show from an outline, using the outline levels as a guide, the first level text is treated as a heading and so on.

For example, if you created an outline within Word you could use this to create a **PowerPoint** presentation without having to retype the text. This works rather effectively and can be a real time-saver.

You can see the results in the next illustration.

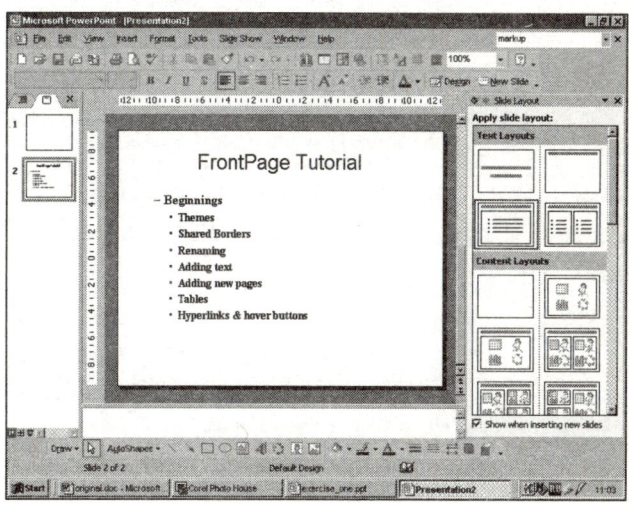

To do this, pull down the **Insert** menu and select **Slides from Outline**. Find the file you want to use and **PowerPoint** will convert it into a presentation. You will then need to make any alterations and to customise the presentation.

Pictures

These are treated in a very similar way to clip art; they can (mostly but not always, depending upon the type of file) be sized, recoloured, grouped and ungrouped and so on.

Scanned images require a large amount of disc space to store and tend to slow the system when used.

A partial fix for this is to scale the scanned image before saving it so that it is the correct size.

However, you should not make it too small as subsequently increasing the size of an image can reduce the definition.

The type of file you save the image as will also affect the file size; some graphic formats create considerably smaller files (sometimes with a loss of quality).

To insert a picture, pull down the **Insert** menu, select **Picture** and then select the type of image from the list.

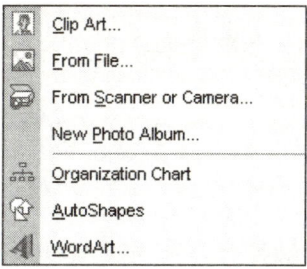

For example, find a picture on your hard disc and **Insert** it into your presentation.

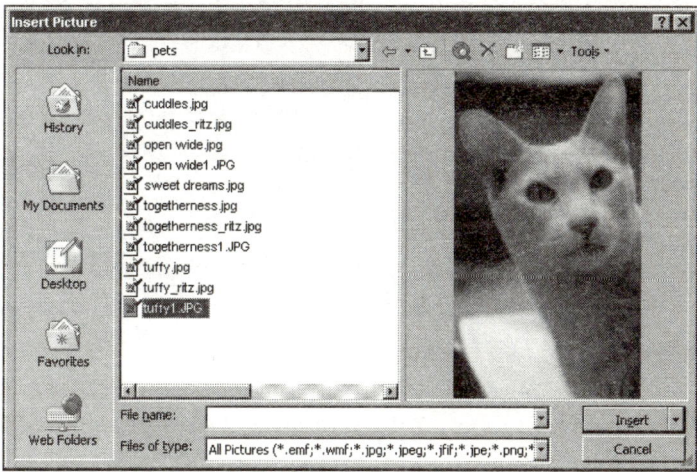

Text Box

To create a textbox click the **Text Box** button (**Drawing** toolbar) and then click and drag to create the box, adding text as desired.

The example below shows a text box to the side of the picture.

Movies and Sounds

Use this option to insert movie clips and sounds. You will see a menu of choices.

To insert a movie, e.g. from the **Clip Organizer**, is similar to any other media. The **Insert Clip Art** pane will be shown on the right side of the window and you can search for movies (which include animations).

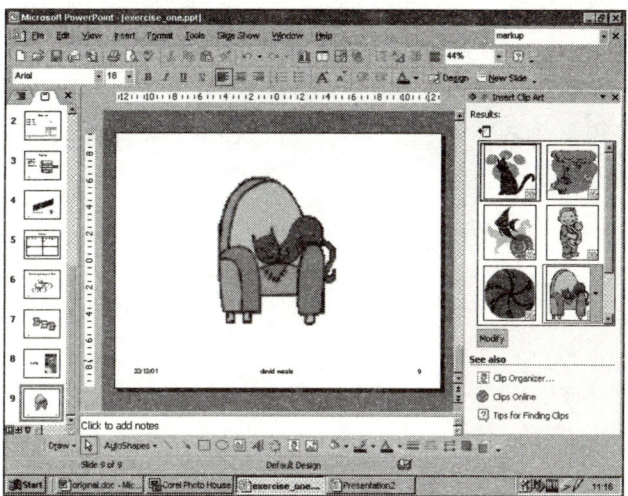

The animation will work when you run the **Slide Show**.

You can add sounds in a similar way. You will be asked whether you want the sound to play automatically or when clicked.

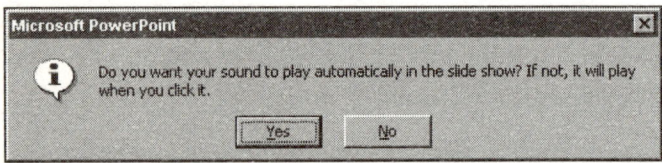

The final illustration shows both a movie clip and sound inserted into a slide, both of which play when you view the slide show.

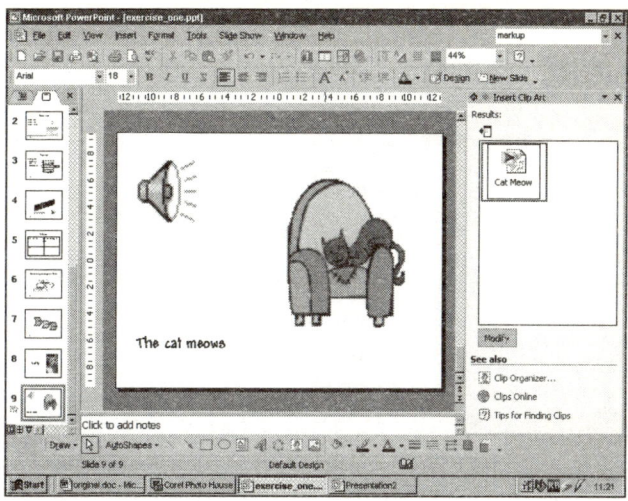

You can change the way in which movies and sounds are played by pulling down the **Slide Show** menu and selecting **Custom Animation**.

Format menu

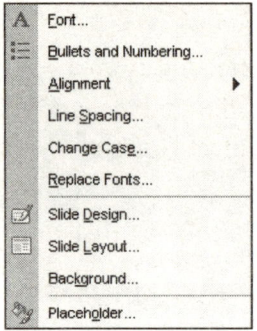

Font

You can alter the font by using the toolbar buttons, however pulling down the **Format** menu and then **Font**, offers more choice.

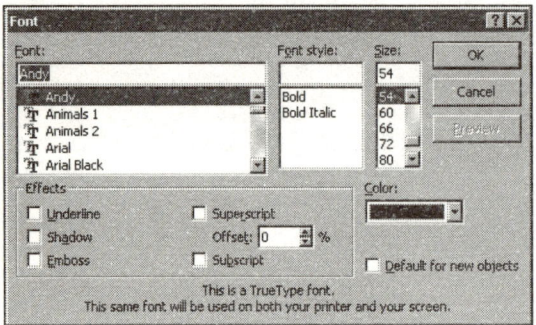

Bullets and Numbering

If you want to alter the predefined bullets (you can make these changes for an individual slide, or for all the slides by altering the **Master Slide**), first select the text for which you want to alter the bullets and then pull down the **Format** menu and select **Bullets**.

There are various options. You can choose bullets from any character set (**Customize**) or a picture (**Picture**).

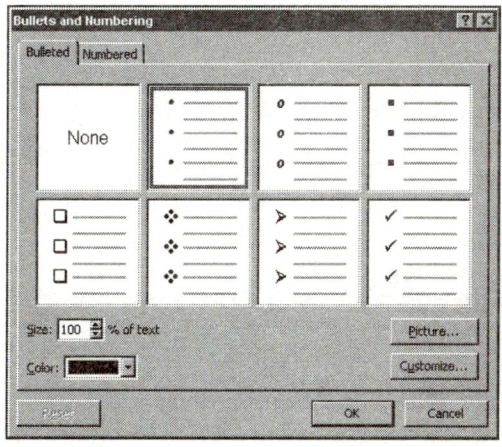

The **Picture** option contains an **Import** button to import any image to use as a bullet.

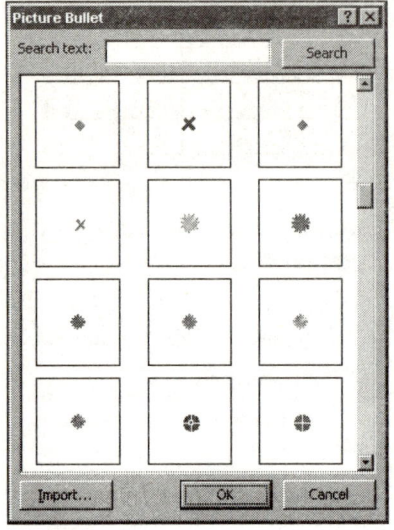

Alignment

To alter the alignment of paragraph(s), highlight the text and then pull down the **Format** menu and select **Alignment**, or use the alignment buttons on the toolbar.

The **Alignment** menu gives more choice (as it includes **Justification**).

Alternatively, you can use the following keys (holding the first down while depressing the latter).

CTRL E	centre
CTRL J	justify
CTRL L	left
CTRL R	right

Line Spacing

Obviously hitting the **Return** key will create space; unfortunately, it will also create another bullet. To avoid this, hold down the **Shift** key while depressing the **Return** key, this is a soft return and does not give rise to a new bullet.

A more satisfactory method to alter the line spacing (for an individual slide or for the master slide) is to use the **Format** menu and then **Line Spacing**.

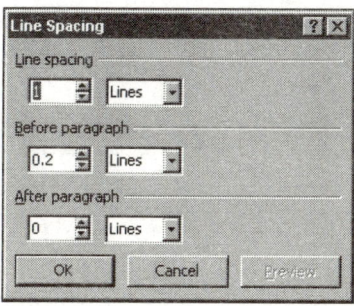

A dialogue box will appear and you can alter the line spacing and the space before and after paragraphs as you wish.

Better still, you will be able to **Preview** the effect on screen as you make the changes.

> Grab the dialogue box and move it out of the way, so that you can see the effect more clearly when you **Preview**.

You **must** highlight the text to alter the line spacing for more than one line.

Change Case

You can change the case of the text you have typed.

Believe me this is very useful; it is very easy to type text with the **Caps Lock** key on by mistake.

To use this feature you need to highlight the text and then pull down the **Format** menu and select **Change Case**.

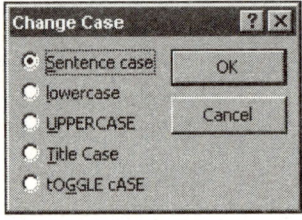

> You can also use **Shift** and **F3** to alter the case of highlighted text.

Replacing Fonts

In the **Format** menu is an option called **Replace Fonts**. This lets you alter one font to another.

The dialogue box is shown below; you can use the arrows to the right of each box to alter the choices.

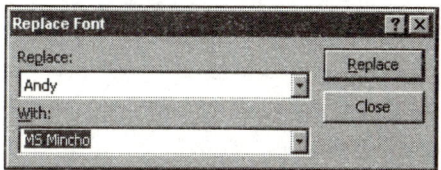

Slide Design

This displays the **Slide Design** pane on the right side of the screen, the same effect can be achieved using the **Design** button on the **Formatting** toolbar.

Background

Pull down the **Format** menu and select **Background**. You will see the following dialogue box.

Choose another colour and **Preview** or **Apply** it to your slides.

Be careful with the buttons **Apply to All** and **Apply**. Your choice will depend upon whether you want to change the background of all the slides or not.

Ticking the **Omit background graphics** option removes any graphics or text that has been included in the **Master Slide**.

Format Text/Object/Picture/Placeholder

This name of this menu option varies with what is selected.

The **Format** dialogue box will be shown, the option within it depending upon the item selected.

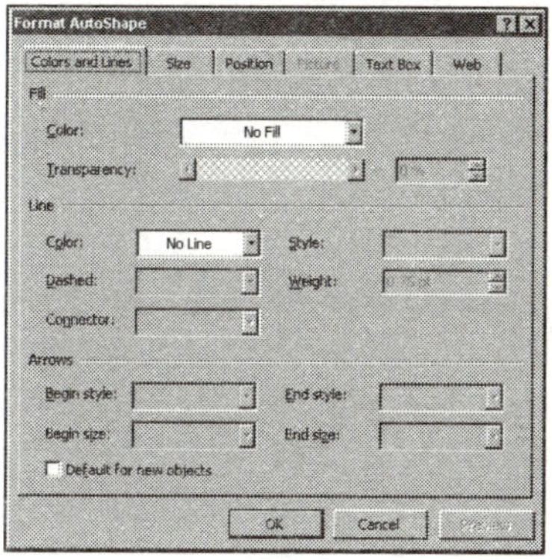

Double-clicking the object or text box will also display this dialogue box.

Format Painter

This button allows you to alter how any text or object appears by copying the attributes (colour, shading, etc.) from one to the other.

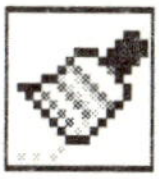

To work with the **Format Painter**, click on the text/object you want to copy the formatting from, then click on the **Format Painter** button and drag the mouse pointer over the text/object to which you want to copy the attributes.

Tools menu

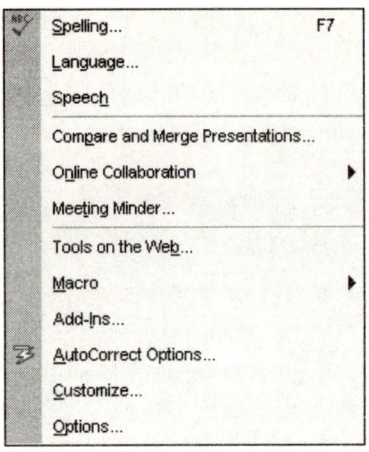

Language

You use this to set the language (for spelling and other checking purposes). The default is the choice of language you made when you installed **Windows** (to alter the default use the **Default** button).

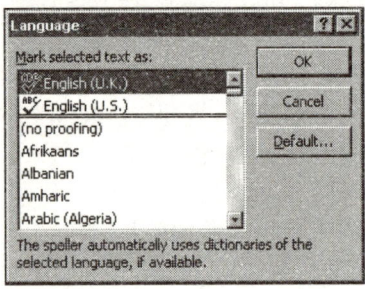

Speech

This new feature uses a microphone and voice recognition software to enter text (it is only available in certain versions of the program).

Compare and Merge Presentations

This works by merging another presentation with the current one. It works with a presentation that has been reviewed by another person (after having been sent to that person using **File**, **Send to**).

After the file has been received back by the sender then the two versions can be compared and merged (any alterations made by the reviewer do not overwrite the original).

After it is returned, a dialogue box appears.

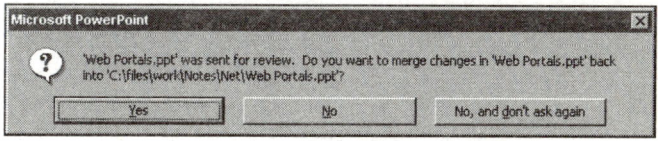

In addition, two versions of the same presentation can be compared (without having been reviewed).

In this case, a different dialogue box appears; click the **Continue** button to compare the presentations.

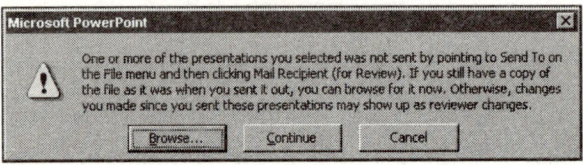

The **Revisions** pane is used to accept or reject changes to the original.

The two versions are compared and the toolbar buttons can be used to vary the presentations, incorporating or removing the revisions as desired.

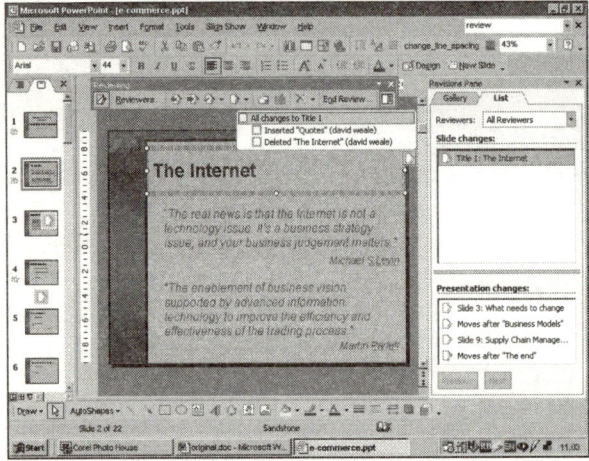

Online Collaboration

This enables you to set up online meetings and to allow people to add comments to your work.

Meeting Minder

This enables you to set up and organise meetings. It requires **Outlook** to be installed in order to allow the meeting to be **Scheduled**.

Tools on the Web

This connects to the **Microsoft** web site and from there to the **Tools on the Web** page.

Macro

A macro (in its simplest form) is a series of commands, keystrokes and other activities. You record this series and then play it back without having to enter the keystrokes individually.

Recording and running a macro

To record a macro you can use the **Macro Recorder**.

Pull down the **Tools** menu, select **Macro**, then **Record New Macro**.

The dialogue box will be displayed. Add the **Macro name** (see illustration below).

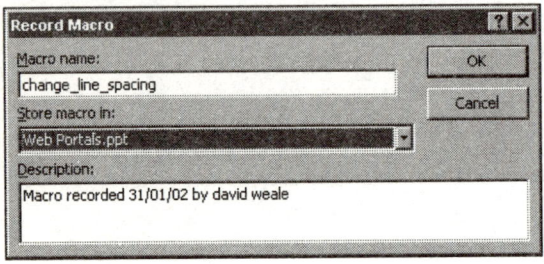

Click **OK** and begin to record the macro (carry out the series of keystrokes you wish to record).

When finished, pull down the **Tools** menu and select **Macro**, followed by **Stop Recording**.

To run the macro, pull down the **Tools** menu, select **Macro** and then **Macros**.

You should see a dialogue box listing the macros.

Select the macro you want to use and click the **Run** button.

> In order to run the macro, the file containing the macro has to be open.

Assigning a macro to a toolbar button

You can assign a macro to a button on any visible toolbar by pulling down the **Tools** menu and selecting **Customize**, followed by **Commands**.

In the **Categories** list find **Macros** and drag the **macro** onto any of the visible toolbars.

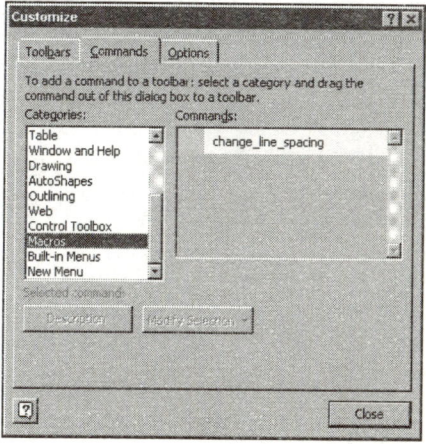

Running a macro during a slide show

On the slide, select the text or object, e.g. an **action button**, you want to use to run the macro.

On the **Slide Show** menu, click **Action Settings**.

In the dialogue box, choose either the **Mouse Click** tab or the **Mouse Over** tab, depending upon how you want the macro to be activated.

Click **Run macro**, and then select the macro you want from the list (the list will only contain macros that have been saved within this presentation file).

Add-Ins

These are additional programs, which enhance the use of **PowerPoint**.

You can obtain add-in programs from a variety of sources, e.g. Microsoft's web site.

AutoCorrect Options

This sets rules for **AutoCorrect**.

You can make any alterations you want, delete rules, add new rules, and create exceptions to the rules and so on.

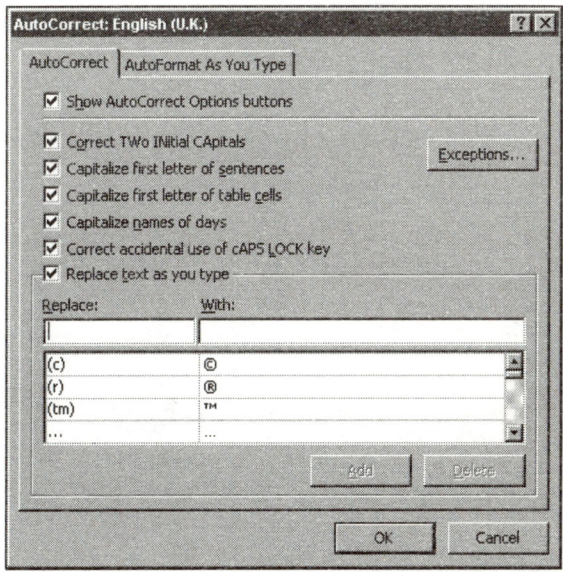

Customize

This enables you to add and delete buttons to reflect the way you personally work.

After pulling down the **Tools** menu, select **Customize** and you will see a dialogue box.

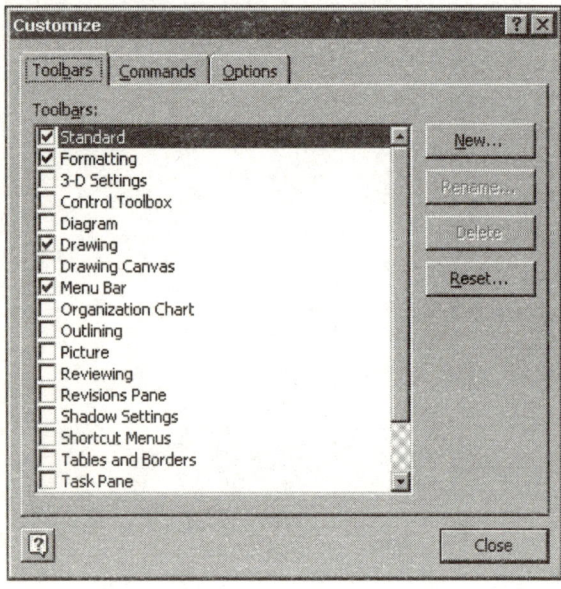

You can select from the different toolbars shown.

Add buttons by selecting the **Commands** tab and then grabbing the button and dragging it to any toolbar on the screen.

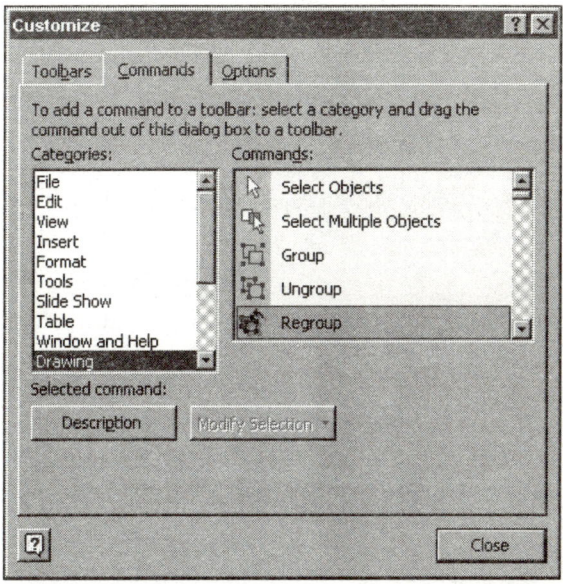

To remove a button, simply drag it off the toolbar.

If you decide that you have made a mess of any toolbar then the **Reset** button on the **Toolbar** menu lets you put everything back to its default position.

Options

In the **Tools** menu is **Options**. This is where various changes to the way the program works can be made.

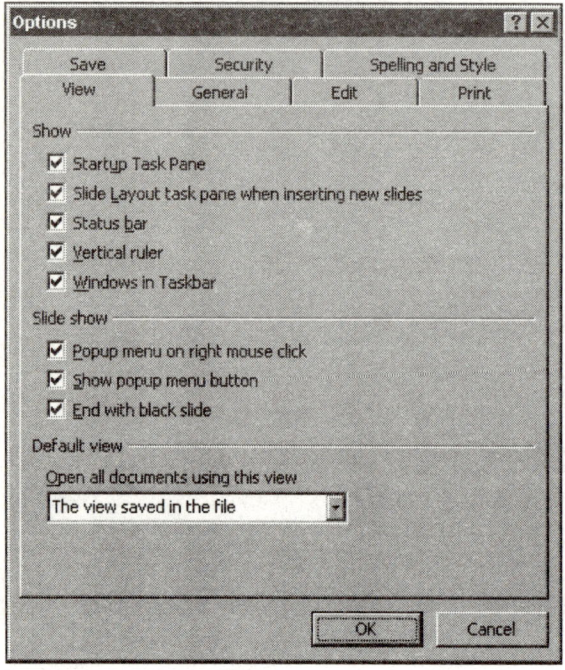

Each of the tabs (**View**, **General**, **Edit**, etc.) contains program settings that you can alter from the default.

Use the program **Help** to learn the effect of any of these.

Slide Show Menu

View Show

This runs the slide show; you can use the **Slide Show** button instead (bottom left of the screen).

Set Up Show

This option gives you various choices on how to run the show.

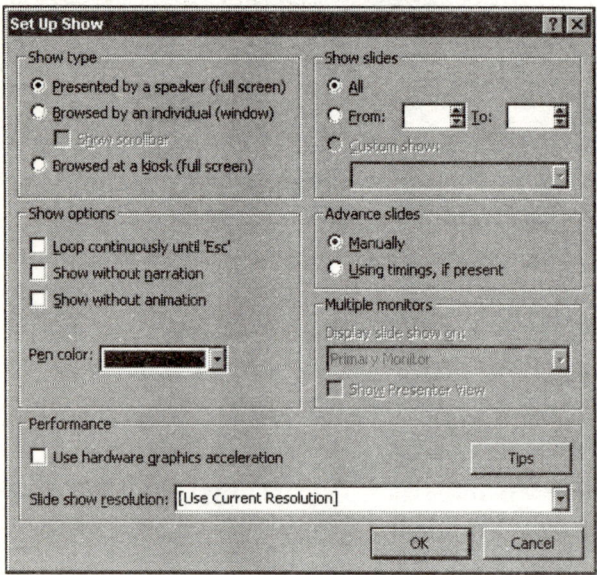

Rehearse Timings

This runs the slide show, rehearsing the timings you have set or you can set timings using this option.

To set timings using the **Rehearse Timings** option, use the dialogue box (shown below).

You can use the arrow symbol to advance the slides and the **Repeat** and **Pause** buttons as appropriate. When you have finished, you will be asked if you want to save the new timings.

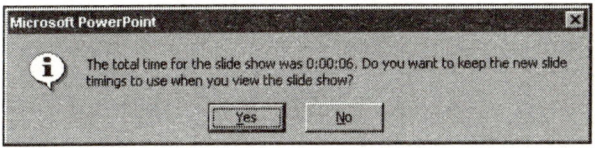

Once you have set the timings, use the **Set Up Show** dialogue box to alter the **Advance slides** to **Using timings, if present**.

Record Narration

If you have a sound card and microphone, you can add a spoken commentary to your slide show.

This can be done while the presentation is running (with audience participation if you wish) or at some other time.

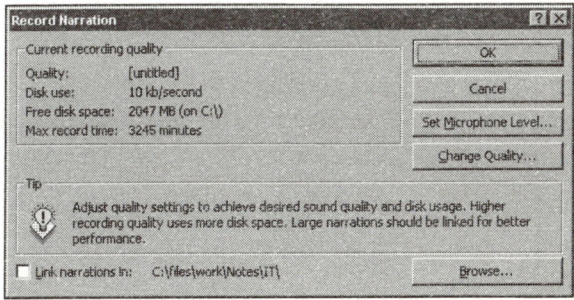

Online broadcast

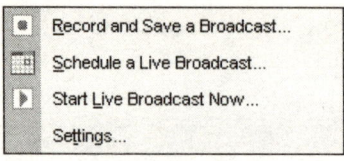

This enables you to broadcast a presentation across a network.

Action Buttons

You can add buttons to your slides, which are activated either by clicking the mouse on them or by moving the mouse over them.

You choose your button from the display and then click and drag the mouse to create the button within the slide.

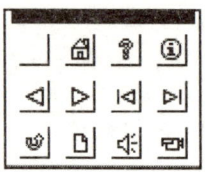

Then you enter the necessary data in the dialogue box that will (automatically) appear.

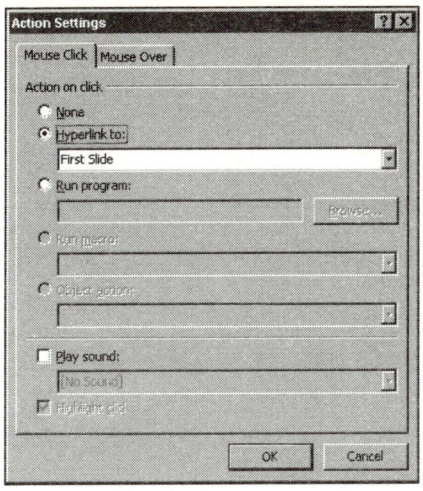

The following illustration shows an action button set to play the sound of applause, so whenever I click on the symbol, there will be the sound of applause.

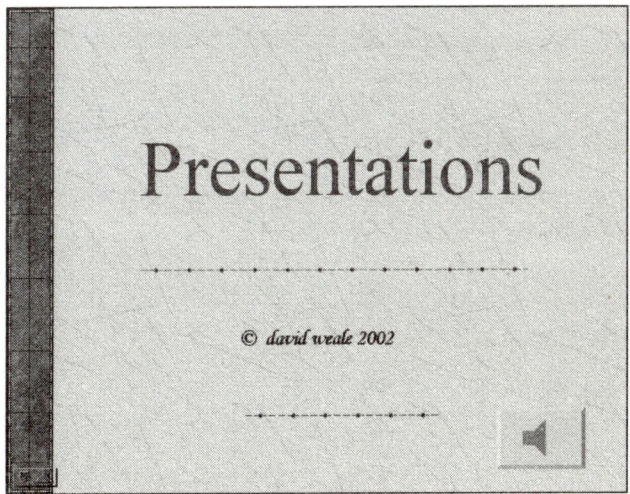

Another use of action buttons is to jump to a **Custom Show** or to another slide show by entering a **Hyperlink** (to another slide, on either the hard disc or an Intranet or the Internet).

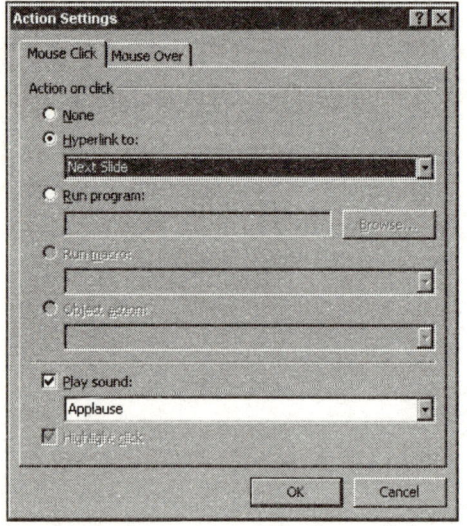

Action Settings

This only becomes available when you have created an action button. You can then alter the settings after selecting the button.

Animation Schemes

This gives you a choice of animations (builds) to apply to your slide show.

Animations are special effects that can be applied to text, graphics, buttons, etc. When you run your slide show, you will see the animation take place.

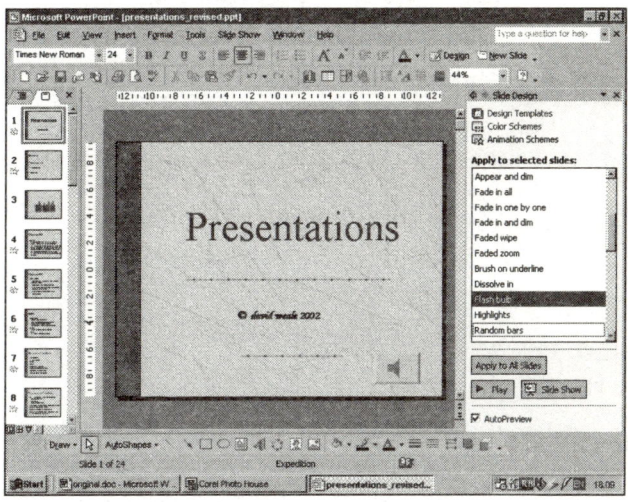

The animation schemes are shown on the right of the screen (**Slide Design** pane), the animation can be applied to all the slides (**Apply to All Slides**) or just to the slide being viewed.

Be warned, too many different animations can lead to the viewer paying more attention to the technique and not enough attention to your message.

Custom Animation

This gives you more control over the animations.

You select which parts of the slide to animate, in what order the animations take place and whether the animation is automatic or on a mouse click.

If you want the same animation effect to appear on every slide, then view the **Master Slide** and apply the required effects.

To apply an animation, firstly select the part of the slide, e.g. the text area, an image, etc.

Click the **Add Effect** button and select the effect you require.

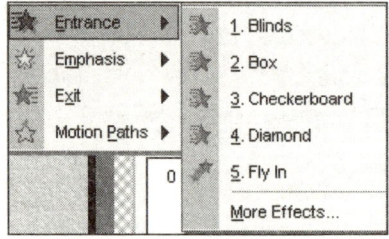

Once an effect has been selected, then various features can be changed, e.g. **Start**, **Speed**, etc.

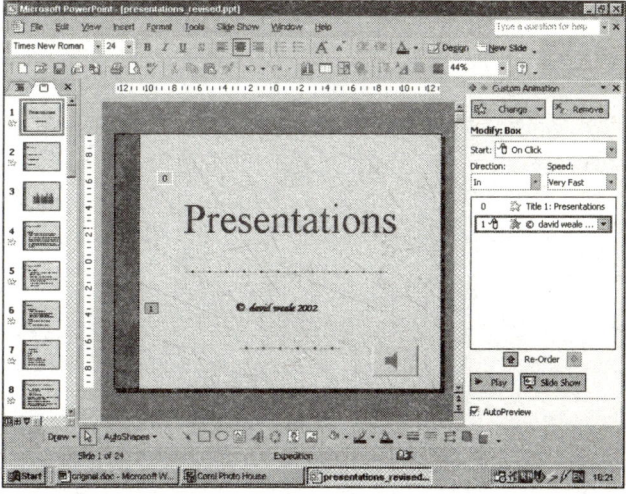

Dimming text

One of the effects is to alter the colour of each line of text (as the next line appears), so that the current point appears in a prominent colour and the previous points are dimmed.

Select the item by clicking it in the **Custom Animation pane** (to select multiple items, hold down the **Ctrl** key and click the mouse).

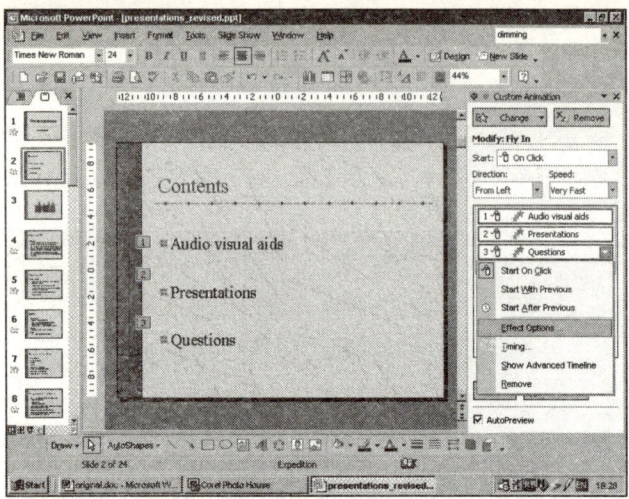

Click the arrow to the right of the item(s), and select **Effect Options** and then **Effect**. Finally, choose the effects, e.g. change the text colour in the **After animation** box.

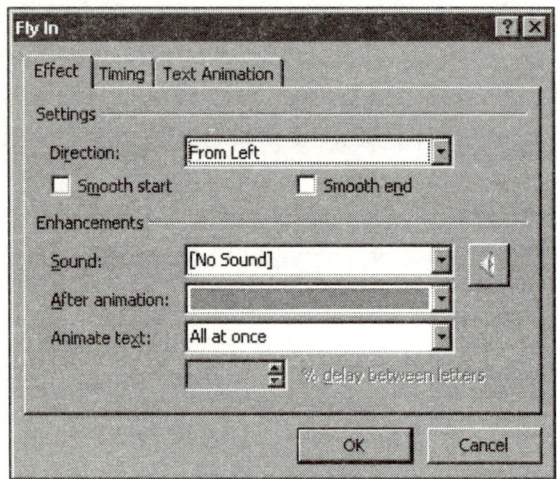

Slide Transition

This is a special effect between each slide, to set this, select the **Slide Show** menu and then **Slide Transition**.

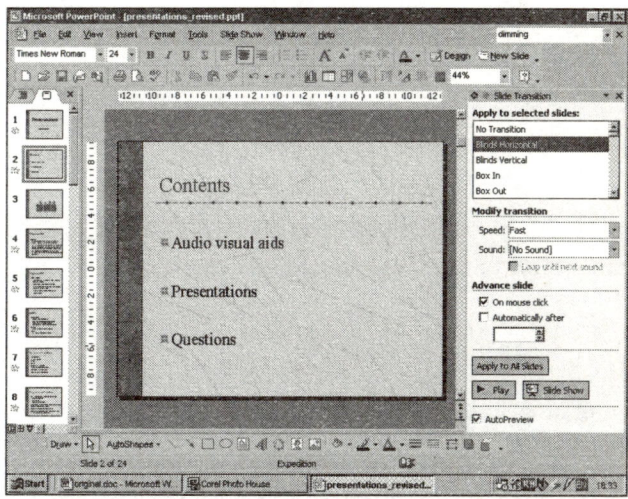

Select the transition from the list and alter the options as you wish. You will see the effect reproduced as you make the changes.

The transition can be applied to all the slides or only to the current slide.

Within this pane, it is possible to set the slide show to run automatically using set timings for the slides **Advance slide** (**Automatically after**), e.g. for an exhibition. The slide timings can also be set manually using the **Set Up Show** option within the **Slide Show** menu.

Hide Slide

You can hide individual slides so that they do not display.

If you are in **Slide Sorter View**, you can select several slides (to select several slides hold down the **Ctrl** key while clicking the mouse pointer on each).

To hide a slide, select the slide(s), pull down the **Tools** menu and select **Hide Slide**, or if you are in **Slide Sorter View** use the **Hide Slide** button (on the upper toolbar).

Displaying Hidden Slides

Type the character **H** while displaying the previous slide.

When printing, the dialogue box is set to print the hidden slides (the default) or by removing the tick, print the slides without including the hidden slide.

Custom Shows

You can build up slide shows that contain (some of the) slides from the original slide show.

You may want to do this because you are dealing with a variety of audiences, which require a different version of the original.

Click on **New** and then you will see the following dialogue box, choose the slides and then **Add** them to the custom show.

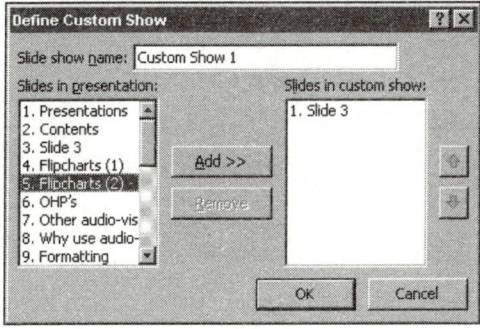

Help menu

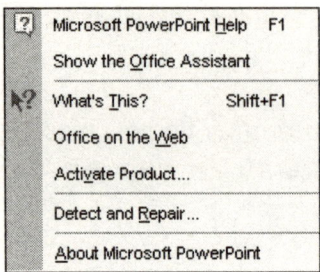

The Office Assistant

The assistant is normally always on screen or can be called from the menu by selecting **Microsoft PowerPoint Help** or by clicking the button on the toolbar.

Choices

After right clicking the mouse button on the assistant and selecting **Options**, a dialogue box appears which enables you to choose a different assistant (**Gallery**).

Alternatively, if you select the **Options** tab, you can make various changes.

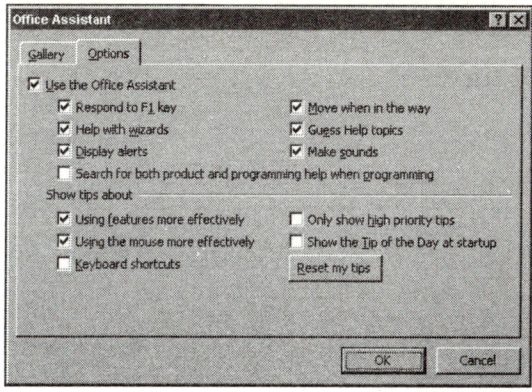

The Search Button

To get an answer to any query, type in a word or phrase and click the **Search** button. The results will be displayed; select which answer is closest and click this, finally arriving at the actual help screen.

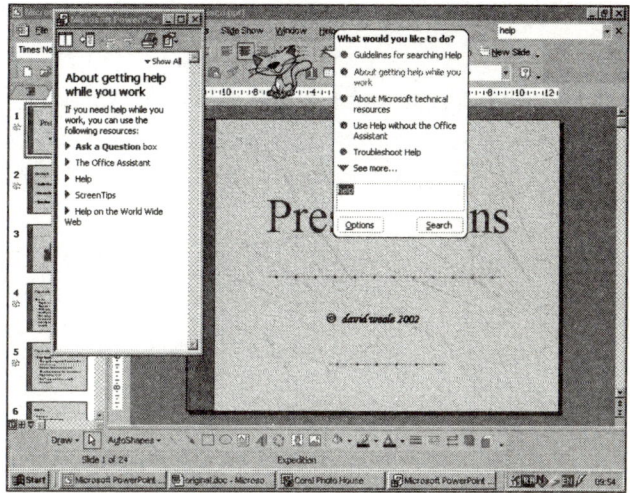

Move around the help screens by clicking the hyperlinks (which are normally in blue).

Note the buttons along the top of the help screen; the second of these is the **Show** button used to display the more traditional method of obtaining help.

The other buttons enable you to move back or forward through the screens you have looked at or to print the text. There is an **Options** button on the far right, which adds certain features.

Using the Show button

As you can see from the illustration, you have the **Contents**, **Answer Wizard** and **Index** options.

Contents

As you can see from the following illustration, the contents are like a series of books or chapters on the various aspects of the program.

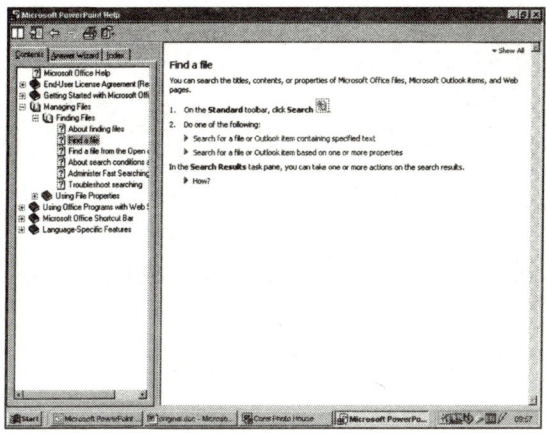

Each book can be opened by double-clicking on it to reveal the sections within that book and each book or chapter can be printed by selecting it and then clicking the **Print** button.

Answer Wizard

Instead of choosing from a list, here you type in the word or phrase and the nearest equivalents are displayed so you can select the one you want. The details are then shown in the right pane.

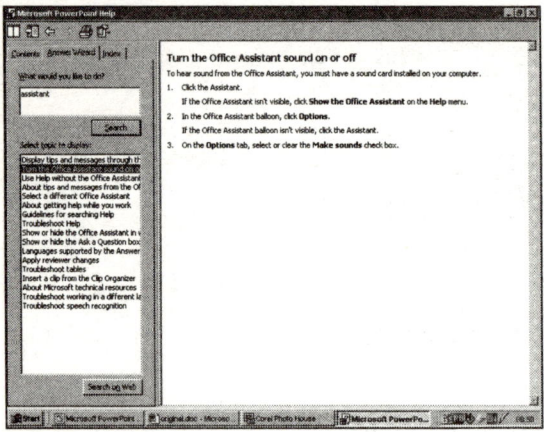

Index

This includes a list of keywords as well as the option of typing a keyword.

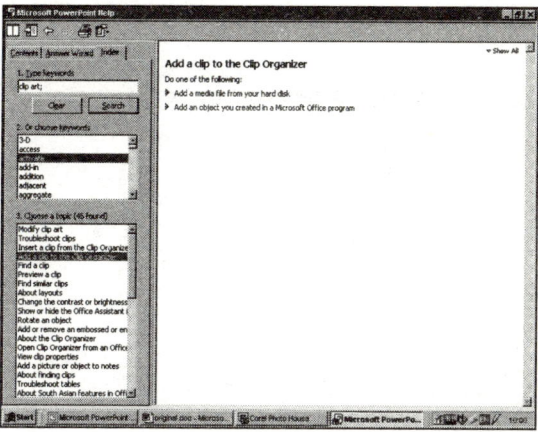

Office on the Web

This option will connect you to the **Microsoft** site on the Internet. Your browser (e.g. **Microsoft Explorer**) will be loaded and so will the site.

Detect and Repair

This enables the program to be repaired (from the original disc).

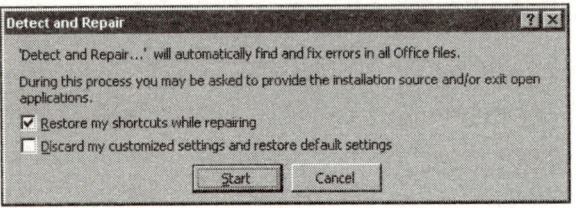

About Microsoft PowerPoint

This displays information about the program.

Advice about presentations

First Things

Decide **WHAT** you want to achieve.

- ☐ Do you want to impart information or to persuade your audience in some way (e.g. to change their beliefs or attitudes)?

- ☐ Consider the type of audience you are addressing and what they want from the presentation. Pitch the level of your presentation carefully; audiences vary in their attention span, intellectual ability, etc.

- ☐ Decide upon the best way to get your message across for the specific audience.

The Material

Write down the main points and then underneath write the detail.

The audience likes to have something to take away, so prepare a handout or copy of the OHPs you have used.

The Presentation

Always introduce the material (subject, contents) and yourself (background, qualifications) to the audience and remember to wrap it all up at the end by summarising what you have told them and ask for questions (unless you want to deal with questions during the presentation – make it clear at the start which method your prefer).

The sequence of the presentation should be logical, starting simply before developing complex points, a presentation is an overview of the subject and it may be preferable to use handouts for complex details.

The start and end of the presentation are critical to its success so pay particular attention to these.

Your voice is of primary importance, keep it slow and interested, emphasise the important points and the changes of topic, this keeps your audience awake.

Try to avoid referring to notes or cue cards, as the audience would prefer if you appeared in command of the subject.

Maintain eye contact with as many of the audience as possible. Always practise, preferably in front of a live audience or video camera.

The audience is most likely to have a worthwhile experience if you exude enthusiasm, seem to be enjoying yourself and (appear to) know your subject.

Consider dress and body language, these can make or mar the overall presentation.

The Environment Itself

Always check the room, seating, lighting and the display equipment (computer, OHP, projector, etc.).

Ensure the image and text are bright, in focus and large enough for everyone to see clearly.

Make sure that all the audience can actually see the screen easily (try not to stand in front of it). Arrange the seating and adjust any other environmental features (heating, lighting, etc.) as necessary.

Using Software

Keep a consistent style throughout the slides. Use clip art, charts or drawings to make points or to amuse but be careful not to detract from the actual message.

Use the design, animation and transition effects to add a degree of professionalism but do be consistent with their use (and any other special effects) as you want the audience to pay attention to the content **not** to the technology.

Keep the slides as simple as possible, too much detail is pointless and counter-productive, the purpose of the slides is to emphasise the main points of your talk not, usually, to replace the talk itself.

Make sure all the audience can read the slides (are the fonts large enough for those at the back of the room).

Slide Layout

Use initial capital letters but then lower case (i.e. not all capitals).

Keep the number of words, lines, numbers or graphic images to the absolute minimum for each slide (the maximum number of lines should ideally not be more than six).

Make sensible use of fonts and remember that you need to use large fonts so that the audience can read them easily without effort. It is likely that font sizes less than 18 points will not be readable, in many cases the larger the text the more effective it will be.

Use **bold**, size and colour to enhance text and use italics sparingly (perhaps for quotes).

Create a professional finish by ending with a blank coloured slide (or a slide with your company logo) and always **Spellcheck**.

Colours and Things
Be careful with your use of colour.

Try to avoid complicated images or backgrounds, as these can be confusing to the audience and detract from the points you are trying to put across.

Be aware of contrasts, dark letters on a light backdrop show up well, charts and diagrams look good with a light (but not too bright) background.

Index

A

Action buttons 138, 140
Action settings 130, 140
Add effect 142
Add-Ins 130
Advanced search 85
Align 72, 118
Animation scheme 16, 141
Answer Wizard 151, 152
Arrows 101
Assign 129
Assistant 148
AutoContent 10
AutoCorrect 131
AutoFormat 56
AutoShape 74

B

Background 122, 156, 159
Body language 157
Body text 33
Bring forward 70
Bring to front 70
Build 21, 147
Bullet 33, 118, 119

C

Change case	120
Clip organizer	39, 113
Clipboard	94
Color scheme	16, 17, 18
Comments	30, 90, 105, 107, 127
Contents	151
Control panel	124
Convert	110
Crop	61
Cue cards	156
Custom animation	115, 142
Custom properties	98
Custom show	23, 140, 147
Customise	2, 83, 110, 132
Cut	93

D

Date	103, 106
Delete	65, 96
Delete slide	12, 20, 65, 96
Details	10, 152
Diagram gallery	52
Distribute	72
Duplicate	96, 106

E

Edit point	74
E-mail	89
End show	27
Environment	157
Equation	57
Excel	43
Explorer	153
Export	24
Eye contact	156

F

Find	97
Find next	97
Flip	73, 74
Flowchart	75
Font size	34, 158
Footer	103, 106
Format painter	123
Frame slides	30
Free rotate	73

G

Gallery	39, 40, 148
General templates	13
Graph	41, 42, 43
Grayscale	99
Grid	71, 102
Group	68, 69, 73
Guides	71, 102

H

Handout	29, 104, 155
Header	103, 106
Help	148
Hidden slides	30, 146
Hide	26, 30, 102, 107, 146
HTML	77, 78
Hyperlink	80, 81, 95, 140

I

Import	43, 118
Index	80, 151, 153, 161
Internet	10, 77, 140, 153
Intranet	10, 140

J

Justification 118

L

Language 124
Large previews 9, 17
Layout 7
Line spacing 119, 120
Link 81, 95

M

Macro 128, 129, 130
Mail 89
Markup 105
Master slide 34, 63, 64, 117, 119, 122, 142
Meeting Minder 24, 127
Merge 68, 125
Microsoft.com 14
Mouse click 130, 142
Mouse over 130, 138
Move 59, 97
Movie 113, 114

N

Narration	137
Navigator	23
Normal view	18, 65
Notes pane	2, 6
Nudge	72

O

Object	59, 61, 73
Office collections	39
OHP	21, 157
Online	24, 127, 138
Options	134
Order	69, 127, 129, 142
Organisation chart	36, 51, 53, 55
Outline pane	2, 4, 15
Outlines	109, 110
Outlook	24, 127

P

Pack and Go 86
Page setup 87
Paste 93, 95
Paste Special 95
Pause 27, 137
Pen 26, 27
Picture 61, 111
Placeholder.. 123
Print.. 28
Print preview 88
Projector.. 21, 157
Properties 92, 98
Publish 79

R

Regroup.. 68
Rehearse Timings 136
Repeat 97, 137
Replace... 97, 121
Reset... 133
Restore panes 6
Revisions.. 126
Rotate 73, 74
Rulers 101

S

Save	31
Save as type	32
Save in	31
Scale	30, 110
Scanned images	110
Schedule	24
ScreenTips	3
Search	38, 40, 85, 97, 113, 149
Send backwards	70
Send to	89, 125
Send to back	70
Set up show	136, 137, 145
Shape	54, 74, 75, 101
Sizing	59, 61
Slide Background	122
Slide Layout	8, 46, 51, 158
Slide master	63
Slide navigator	23
Slide show	21
Slide sorter	18, 20, 21, 65, 96, 108, 146
Snap	71
Sounds	40, 113, 114, 115
Spacing	119, 120
Speaker notes	25
Speech	125
Spellcheck	159

Spelling 35
Statistics 92
Structure 80
Style 44, 63, 157
Symbol 51, 75, 107, 112, 137, 139

T

Tables 36, 46, 49
Task pane 2, 5, 6, 7, 9, 13, 94
Template 8
Text box 38, 66, 107, 112, 123
Timings 27, 136, 137, 145
Title 23, 54, 63, 95
Toolbar 6, 31, 133
Toolbar options 2
Transition 21, 145, 158

U

Undo 96
Ungroup 67, 68, 73

V

Video 36, 40, 156
View datasheet 41
View show 135
Viewer 86, 95, 142

W

Web 77, 78, 79, 80, 81, 95, 130, 153
Web Page 10
Web page preview 79, 87
Web sites 13, 95
Wizard 10, 12, 151, 152
WordArt 36, 44, 45, 59

Z

Zoom 19

Notes

Notes

Notes

Notes

Notes

Notes

Notes

Notes